American Foreign Relations

IN THE TWENTIETH CENTURY

Documents Selected and Edited by

MANFRED JONAS

Union College

D1305983

Thomas Y. Crowell Company / *New York* / *Established 1834*

PRESENTED TO

BAPTIST BIBLE COLLEGE

RICHARD J. MURPHY

MEMORIAL LIBRARY

BY

Mr. Jim Huckaby
BBC Faculty

American Foreign Relations

IN THE TWENTIETH CENTURY

Crowell Source Readers in American History

DAVID BRODY, *General Editor*

The purpose of this series is to provide students of American history
with a means for approaching key problems through the evaluation of
the historical evidence. Each of the volumes in the series concentrates
on several major issues relating to one area of American history. The
editors have chosen documents that focus on those issues in an
immediate way and from a variety of contemporary standpoints.
Each section contains a solid body of evidence for the study of the
topic being covered. Introductory essays that set the issues in their
historical context are included in each volume and each section is
preceded by a headnote that relates each document to the theme of
the section. The objective of this series will be fulfilled if the student
is enabled to think independently about the issues contained in these
volumes. The titles in the series are *American Foreign Relations in the
Twentieth Century*, edited by Manfred Jonas; *American Thought in
the Twentieth Century*, edited by David Van Tassel; *The American
South in the Twentieth Century*, edited by Robert L. Brandfon; *Industrial
America in the Twentieth Century*, edited by David Brody; and,
forthcoming, *Urban America in the Twentieth Century*, edited by
Milton Spiezman, and *American Politics in the Twentieth Century*,
edited by John Braeman.

To the Memory of MY FATHER

Preface

No brief collection of readings, however judiciously chosen, can hope to convey adequately the scope and complexity of American foreign relations in the twentieth century. The selections brought together here fulfill the less ambitious function of providing a coherent picture of the main lines along which the foreign policy of the United States has developed over the last seventy years. Generous samplings of the words of major policymakers and of their leading critics have been included, in order to show not only the outlines of the policy itself but also the reasoning behind it and the arguments against it. Preference has been given to selections that incorporate the speaker's or writer's view of the world and of America's place in the world.

I am grateful for the assistance rendered by Ruth Anne Evans and Charles F. Wilde of the Schaffer Library of Union College, and owe a special debt to Nancy Petersen Gibbons and Susan Peters, whose skills were essential to the preparation of the manuscript.

M.J.

Schenectady, N. Y.
March, 1967

Contents

Introduction

I T IS scarcely an exaggeration to say that during the first century of its existence the United States had no foreign policy at all. As a country of little economic and no military importance, without strong neighbors, protected by wide expanses of ocean and the polar icecap, and favored by a world balance of power which tended in most instances to safeguard its interests, America could afford the luxury of devoting its attention almost exclusively to domestic problems. Its relationship with other nations was based in large measure on the essentially negative precepts of Washington, Jefferson, and Monroe: avoidance of permanent entangling alliances, noninterference in European affairs, and opposition to European intervention in the Western Hemisphere. Unallied and uncommitted, and threatened neither by invasion nor loss of territory, the United States was able to act independently and at its own discretion in those rare cases in which events elsewhere in the world seemed to affect the nation's interests.

The peculiar combination of circumstances which had permitted such a course ceased to exist at the close of the nineteenth century. The tremendous growth of industrial and agricultural production after the Civil War, together with the consequent increase in foreign trade and the beginning of investment abroad, made the United States an important factor in the world economy by the 1890's. The need for the protection of trade and investments, as well as the chauvinistic search for the sinews and sym-

1

bols of power, caused America to build a large navy and thus to make itself into a military factor. Advances in the technology of transportation and communication began to shrink the oceans, and the nineteenth-century balance of power, which, for all the abuse heaped on it by American statesmen, had served this country well, was upset by the simultaneous rise to international prominence of Germany and Japan. At the same time, the imperialist fever that seized all of the major powers in the 1870's and raged uncontrolled well into the twentieth century threatened to infect the self-confident new giant of the New World.

I

The change which these developments produced in the foreign relations of the United States was specifically triggered by the Spanish-American War. That "splendid little war," which deserves hardly more than passing mention in the annals of military history, was the first major step in America's rise to world power. Begun out of sympathy for the cause of Cuban independence, out of outrage at the atrocities being committed just ninety miles from the American coast, and out of concern for American investments and trade, the war resulted in the annexation of Puerto Rico and the Philippines, America's only important colonial possessions. It gave the United States a tangible stake in the Caribbean and the Far East and thus created the need for a positive foreign policy.

The immediate issue raised by the Spanish-American War was that of expansion itself. Since the war had not been fought for territorial gain, the question of whether the fruits of victory ought to be retained aroused serious debate. The anti-imperialists not only argued that the governing of colonial peoples tended to undermine America's democratic institutions but also pointed out correctly that such a course would require a radical departure from traditional foreign-policy concepts. The nationalist-imperialists denied both of these assertions and insisted that the United States could move out into the world arena without sacrificing its independence in foreign affairs and without involving itself in the disputes of other nations. Acting on this assumption, they carried the day by proclaiming that the United States, like any great power, had to expand or perish, that its economy needed raw materials and markets which were likely to be pre-empted by others if this country failed to act, and that Anglo-Saxon America had a clear duty to bring to less fortunate peoples the blessings of its democratic institutions, its Christian religion, and its economic skills.

By 1901 the United States was firmly committed to an imperialist course and now faced the problem of adapting its foreign policy to that fact. Both Presidents Theodore Roosevelt and William Howard Taft, however, acted in the comforting belief that the new commitments assumed by the United States altered only the scope, but not the nature, of American foreign policy. They continued to pay homage to Washington, Jefferson, and Monroe and to pursue a policy of independence in world affairs.

In the Caribbean the United States proceeded to establish a sphere of influence after having won, by the Hay-Pauncefote Treaty of 1901, the implicit permission of Great Britain, the only power which might have contested such a step. It retained control over the foreign affairs of Cuba, eliminated an Anglo-German-Italian threat to Venezuela, and helped establish an independent Panama. It set up naval bases in Cuba and the Canal Zone, claimed, through the Roosevelt Corollary to the Monroe Doctrine, to exercise an international police power over the area, and intervened with its military forces in Santo Domingo, Cuba, Nicaragua, Haiti, and Mexico. Where Roosevelt explicitly sanctioned the use of force, Taft sought to rely on "dollar diplomacy," the stimulation of American investments to obviate the need for military intervention. Woodrow Wilson disassociated himself both from intervention and dollar diplomacy. Yet he too, by means scarcely distinguishable from those used by his predecessors, continued to follow what had become the established policy: the unilateral safeguarding of the Caribbean by the United States, both against internal unrest in the countries of the area and the threat of foreign, mainly German, intervention.

In the Far East the United States, again acting alone, attempted to destroy the spheres of influence of other powers.

Through the unilaterally promulgated open-door policy it sought to retain access to the raw materials and markets of China. At the same time, it tried to prevent the domination of the area by a single great power. When Russian expansion threatened to result in such domination, Roosevelt encouraged Japan in its war against the tsarist empire. Yet when Japan had won, he promoted a peace treaty designed to keep the two powers carefully balanced against each other. In subsequent negotiations with a Japan which felt itself cheated of the fruits of victory, the United States adhered to the policy of limiting Japanese power. Furthermore, it sought, through the application of dollar diplomacy to China, to establish American presence in the area more firmly, at least in part as a counterweight to the ambitions of both Japan and Russia.

In the Caribbean American policy remained unchallenged by any major power and was successful in attaining its basic objective. In the Far East, on the other hand, the United States could not make its policy effective without a far greater degree of cooperation with other powers than it was willing to accept. Still, in the first years of the century, the United States seemed to have accomplished what the proponents of imperialism had urged: it had taken an active role in world affairs, expanded and protected its overseas interests, and made its voice heard in the counsels of nations without entering into formal alliances or otherwise limiting its freedom of action.

II

Though the United States had taken a hand in the calling of the Algeciras Conference, which in 1906 resolved the Franco-German dispute over Morocco, had participated in the Hague Peace Conferences of 1899 and 1907, and had greatly enlarged its economic and diplomatic contacts with the great powers prior to 1914, its attention was focused primarily on the Caribbean and the Far East. The outbreak of the First World War confronted this country for the first time with the problem of how a major power can avoid being drawn into a general war. The immediate reaction was automatic. President Wilson issued a declaration of neutrality and asked Americans to be neutral in word and deed. But the same factors which had initially propelled this country into world affairs worked to bring it ultimately into the European war.

The fact that neither side in the conflict posed a direct military threat to the United States and that no tangible American interest appeared to be at stake in the struggle made American neutrality seem not only wise but possible. When both sides violated American maritime rights, the United States protested to Great Britain and Germany. Yet, if indifference to the outcome of a foreign war is an essential ingredient of neutrality, as President Wilson assumed, the United States was never really neutral. The vast majority of Americans regarded Great Britain and France as the standard-bearers of democracy in Europe and Germany as a hotbed of bellicose nationalism, militarism, and autocracy. Germany, moreover, had demonstrated its contempt for human life by submarine attacks on passenger liners. Great Britain was, at worst, guilty of destroying American property, a matter which could be settled in postwar negotiations. The natural result was an unneutral attitude, reflected in a general American preference for an Allied victory.

But not only an emotional attachment to the Allied cause developed early. The World War Allies were America's natural trading partners, who, even in 1912, had purchased 65 percent of American exports and supplied over half of American imports. America's economic commitment to the Allied cause, which increased as the war progressed, was thus not the result of ideological commitment and still less the result of the malevolent greed of bankers and businessmen. It was rather the natural outgrowth of America's traditional trading pattern, modified only in degree by the British blockade and the overall increase in foreign trade.

America's traditional sense of mission added a final dimension to this country's posture with regard to the World War. By 1915 Woodrow Wilson was convinced that the United States should use its new power to help establish a rational system of international relations which would make general wars, if not impossible, at least unlikely in the future. This thought underlay his efforts to secure a negotiated peace and, when these efforts failed, convinced him that a new and peaceful world order could be achieved only after an Allied victory and at a peace conference in which the United States was a respected participant. When the March Revolution in Russia seemed to make the war clearly one of democracy versus autocracy and when Germany deliberately challenged the United States through the resumption of unrestricted submarine warfare, Wilson called on the American people to go to war in order to make the world safe for democracy.

Though there was considerable opposition to America's participation in the war, there can be little doubt that the decision to intervene had majority support. Most Americans did not regard it as a reversal of traditional American policy, for it seemed to them that the United States was merely rising to the defense of its own interests, which would be threatened by a victorious Germany. When Wilson returned from Paris, however, with a treaty that seemed to mock the idealism with which the United States had entered the war and with a proposal for a League of Nations which provided for the kind of permanent entanglement against which Washington and Jefferson had warned, determined opposition developed. The United States was not yet ready to assume the burdens of power, and most Americans were yet unwilling to admit that the new status of their country carried with it duties and responsibilities which ran counter to America's traditional conception of its role in the world.

III

America's participation in the First World War and the subsequent failure to join the League of Nations illustrate the paradox of United States policy in the interwar years. All of the factors which propelled this country into world affairs after 1898 and into war in 1917 became stronger and more compelling through the wartime experience. The United States had now fully demonstrated its previously untested military prowess and given a much clearer indication than ever before of its economic potential. It emerged from the war, moreover, as the world's leading creditor nation and virtually as the world's leading naval power. As a result, this country was more than ever a decisive force in world affairs, and this was reflected in the Washington Conference of 1921, in increasing participation in the nonpolitical work of the League of Nations, in the sending of observers to Geneva, in the seating of American justices on international tribunals, and in the unofficial American efforts, by Charles G. Dawes and later by Owen D. Young, to straighten out the tangled world economic situation by solving the problem of German reparations. It was decisively shown in 1929, when the New York stock market crash triggered a world-wide depression.

Yet if the First World War made the United States a more important factor in world affairs, it also provided the American people with an object lesson on the dangers of international commitment. The fact that the world had neither been rid of war nor made safe for democracy seemed to demonstrate the futility of meddling in European affairs, and various ills to which the United States was prey during the interwar years, particularly and illogically the Depression itself, could be blamed on America's failure to heed the advice of the Founding Fathers to stay at home and to till its own garden. As a result, American policy became one of recognizing international complications without accepting international responsibilities. Secretaries of State Charles Evans Hughes, Frank B. Kellogg, Henry L. Stimson, and Cordell Hull all operated in a world-wide theater and recognized that their actions in Washington had repercussions in London, Paris, Berlin, and Tokyo. But the American government was not prepared to use this fact energetically in the achievement of specific aims. Typical of the American posture during these years was the Pact of Paris, which Secretary Kellogg launched in 1928 and for which he was awarded the Nobel Peace Prize. The pact, ultimately signed by sixty-two nations, rejected war as an instrument of national policy and thus "outlawed" it. But it did not commit the United States to any enforcement action against violators and thus to no specific intervention in world affairs.

The most serious challenge to America's ambivalent posture arose in the early 1930's, when the actions of Germany, Italy, and Japan raised the specter of another general war. Caught up in

the overwhelming domestic problems of the Depression and dis-
illusioned by its failure to save the world in 1917–18, the United
States sought refuge in an isolationism which once again placed
a premium on the unilateral determination of American foreign
policy and set the avoidance of war as the major foreign policy
goal. The so-called neutrality legislation of these years was intended to keep America out of entanglements and war by re-
stricting trade and financial dealings with belligerents. But even
in the Italo-Ethiopian War of 1935–36 and in the Spanish Civil
War which broke out in the latter year, it became clear that far
from disentangling the United States, such legislation only demonstrated the degree of American involvement in world affairs.
Not only did America's stated refusal to participate in future wars
encourage aggressors, the limitations on trade and loans affected
the various sides in the conflicts unequally and thus became, in
themselves, factors in "European" and "Asian" wars. By late 1937
President Roosevelt began at least to consider the idea that American intervention, hopefully short of war, might again be required
to restore law and order on the international scene.

IV

The outbreak of the war in Europe on September 1, 1939, posed
fewer problems for America's foreign-policy makers than might
be supposed. Unlike 1914, when the war had come as a complete
surprise to the United States, Hitler's invasion of Poland began
a conflict long regarded as probable by many Americans. Neutrality was declared at once, but the wisdom of America's staying
out of war, which was accepted as axiomatic at the start of the
First World War, had already been seriously questioned prior
to the outbreak of the Second. Thus, although the prevailing
mood still favored the policies advocated by the isolationists,
this mood did not prevail for long.

The success of Hitler's blitzkrieg against Poland raised fears
for the safety of the United States, and Congress, which had
refused to repeal the arms embargo in July of 1939, repealed it
by a large majority in November. This step marked the beginning of a rather rapid dismantling of the isolationist structure.

The "Great Debate" which accompanied this dismantling can be regarded as the isolationists' swan song. Roosevelt increasingly favored aid to the Allies, still hopefully short of war, and world events strengthened his hand. The die was cast in June 1940 when the fall of France made an Axis victory appear imminent. In September of that year the first peacetime selective service act in American history was passed, and in March 1941 the Lend-Lease Act converted the United States into "the great arsenal of democracy."

The decision to support the Allies was a major shift in American foreign policy, representing as it did a belated commitment to the principle of collective security. This, in turn, led to a hardening of America's position vis-à-vis Japan and ultimately to the Pearl Harbor attack. Once the United States was in the war, the commitment was broadened to cover collective arrangements designed not only to achieve victory, but also to create a viable, peaceful postwar order. As early as January 1, 1942, the Declaration of the United Nations put this country on the path which it had refused to follow in 1919. In numerous wartime statements by the President, by Secretary of State Hull, and by other officials, it was made abundantly clear that the United States was fully prepared to embrace the principle of collective security and to participate, without serious reservations, in the successor organization to the League of Nations.

America's wartime foreign policy, and the plans then made for a postwar policy, rested on two basic assumptions. First, it was believed that the only serious danger to international peace came from Germany, Italy, and Japan, countries which had warlike propensities and had come under the control of outlaw governments. The unconditional surrender of these nations and their conversion, through education and control, into peace-loving states was therefore regarded as the *sine qua non* of a peaceful world. Secondly, it was assumed that all of the nations allied against the Axis would be willing to cooperate in the setting up of an international organization equipped with power to settle international disputes. In line with these assumptions, the major foreign policy goals of the United States became the complete defeat of the Axis powers and the maintenance of the Grand

Alliance. American statesmen devoted themselves wholeheartedly
to the attainment of these goals between 1941 and 1945.

The Yalta Conference was a major effort to attain these goals.
By extracting from the Soviet Union pledges for participation in
the United Nations Organization, for entry into the war against
Japan, and for the establishment of democratic governments in
the areas liberated by the Red Army, it was hoped, though no
longer firmly believed, that America's wartime and postwar objectives might be attained.

V

The failure of the Soviet Union to abide by significant portions
of the Yalta Agreement and the subsequent failure of the Potsdam Conference began a new reassessment of American foreign
policy. The defeat of the Axis powers, it appeared, had not ended
threats to world peace, nor indeed could the wartime cooperation among the Allies be maintained. Even more fundamentally,
the whole principle of collective security, which the United
States had finally embraced after a long struggle, proved inap-
plicable to the postwar world. The Soviet Union now placed its
faith in the extension of its sphere of control along lines dictated
by geopolitical theory, and the other states of Europe were too
weakened to share in the burdens of world leadership. The
United States thus found itself forced to choose between yielding
to the Soviet Union and consciously assuming sole leadership of
what came to be called the free world.

The Truman Doctrine of March 12, 1947, and the Marshall
Plan, first suggested by Undersecretary of State Dean Acheson
on May 8 of that year, marked the second basic change in
America's role in world affairs: from isolationism to collective
security to world leadership. Both proposals reflected the new
policy of containment which George F. Kennan had worked out
in Moscow, and both indicated a willingness to accept the risks
involved in throwing down the gauntlet to the Soviet Union.
The Berlin Blockade of 1948–49 and the outbreak of the Korean
War the following year clarified the nature and extent of these
risks and produced a flurry of what was called neo-isolationism.

In fact, however, the United States did not seriously contemplate retreating to its pre-World War II position. In 1949 it confirmed its commitment to Europe by the establishment of a full-fledged military alliance, the North Atlantic Treaty Organization.

By concentrating its efforts on frustrating Russian expansion in Europe and the Middle East, the United States dramatically shifted the traditional geographic focus of its foreign policy. Both the Communist takeover in China and the outbreak of the Korean War raised questions about the wisdom of this shift. In 1954, after the French had been driven out of Indochina, this country, therefore, moved to strengthen its military commitments in Asia by setting up the Southeast Asia Treaty Organization and the ANZUS Pact and by entering into bilateral agreements with South Korea, the Republic of China, and the Philippines. Shortly thereafter, the United States pledged itself to the support of the government established in South Vietnam.

By 1955, therefore, the United States had assumed world-wide economic and military commitments designed to block further expansion of the Communist world in accordance with the containment doctrine. This policy proved successful in Europe and showed some promise of success in Asia, but it did not seem to provide the means for ending the costly and unnatural "Cold War," which had prevented the conclusion of a peace treaty with Germany, produced a new arms race, and kept the world in a constant state of tension. The result was increasing dissatisfaction with the containment policy.

Four alternatives to this policy were at least theoretically possible. One was a massive effort to win the Cold War, to roll back the Iron Curtain by liberating the so-called captive peoples of Eastern Europe and encouraging an invasion of the Chinese mainland by Chiang Kai-shek's forces. A second possibility involved the achievement of a general detente through compromise. Although the United Nations had proved itself incapable of settling major international disputes, a third alternative involved attempts to strengthen that organization. Finally, consideration was given simply to making the Cold War less burdensome to the United States by greater reliance on weapons of massive retaliation. The first and last of these alternatives were never really tried. Attempts at a detente led to the Geneva Summit Conference of 1955 and the resultant ephemeral "Spirit of Geneva." The United Nations, despite the "uniting for peace" resolution of 1950 which sought to bypass the Security Council in certain cases, demonstrated once again during the crisis produced by the Hungarian uprising of 1956 its inability to effectively counter the actions of a major power. The Cold War thus continued for most of the 1950's, and a Cold War psychology came to dominate American thinking on foreign policy.

VI

The visit of Soviet Premier Khrushchev to the United States in 1959 symbolized the beginning of a new era in international relations. The change in leadership in the Soviet Union and the increasingly obvious Sino-Soviet rift which followed ended at least the first phase of the Cold War by stabilizing Russian-American relations and offering the possibility for a general settlement. The Eisenhower Administration attempted to take advantage of this new situation in its last years, both through new high-level negotiations and new encouragement of the United Nations. President Kennedy entered office with high hopes for a general detente negotiated by the United States and the Soviet Union.

These hopes were soon dashed. A series of crises in Cuba, the Congo, and Vietnam, as well as the building of the Berlin Wall and the Chinese threat against India, made fundamental changes in foreign policy impossible and encouraged continued reliance on the established Cold War reflexes. The inadequacy of these reflexes for dealing with a new and highly complex international situation has produced the continuing debate over American foreign policy which has so far characterized the 1960's.

A relatively small but vocal element in the United States has castigated what it calls a "no-win" policy and, encouraged by the apparent American success during the Cuban Missile Crisis of 1962, has urged the use of force and the threat of force to achieve a world settlement on terms favorable to the United

States. Though their reasoning is not wholly unrelated to that of the old isolationists, the policy these men advocate represents the other extreme from traditional isolationism, i.e., the imposition of a Pax Americana, by force if necessary.

An equally small, though perhaps even more vocal, element has argued that the Communist threat to the United States has been exaggerated and that this country has permitted itself to be maneuvered into morally and militarily untenable positions, particularly in Asia, as a result of continued adherence to what they regard as the outworn clichés of the Cold War. Basing their arguments on the notion that the United States is overcommitted, they urge a complete re-evaluation of American foreign policy goals and development of a new policy designed to achieve more limited objectives.

The men who actually make America's foreign policy have walked a difficult and narrow path between these two alternatives. Rejecting the first as too dangerous and the second as unrealistic, they have attempted to use limited force and a limited threat of force as devices for achieving conditions in which negotiations leading to the settlement of outstanding international problems become possible. Ironically, the great tests of American policy have come in the Caribbean and the Far East, the areas in which the United States launched its first real experiments in the making of foreign policy at the turn of the century. And in these unstable areas of the world neither present policy nor the various alternatives which have been proposed offer solid assurances of success in the foreseeable future.

PART I

The United States Becomes a World Power

(1898–1912)

PRESIDENT McKinley's reluctantly reached decision to intervene in the Cuban war for independence from Spain (Selection 1) revived the smoldering question of whether or not the United States ought to acquire overseas possessions. The anti-imperialists argued that to transform the United States into a colonial power would not only mean abandonment of the traditional foreign policy based on the nonentanglement principle, but would also bring massive and wholly undesirable domestic consequences in its wake (Selection 2). Their argument proved to be less persuasive than that of the nationalist-imperialists who saw the acquisition of colonies as a new fulfillment of America's manifest destiny and who believed that the United States could vastly increase its role in world affairs without sacrificing the unilateralism in foreign relations which had proven so beneficial during the nineteenth century (Selection 3).

Both the exercise of an international police power relying on actual or threatened military intervention (Selection 4) and the subsequent dollar diplomacy relying on economic intervention (Selection 5) were attempts to meet America's new international problems within the traditional foreign-policy framework. They enjoyed short-term success in the Caribbean area, where Great Britain, the only major power with significant territorial and economic interests, voluntarily relinquished its previously dominant role. They were far less successful in the Far East, where all of the major powers had jealously guarded spheres of influence.

As long as the United States did not become directly involved in European rivalries, however, the long-term consequences of trying to meet twentieth-century problems with nineteenth-century methods did not become apparent. The full implications of America's new power and new world role were not reflected, therefore, in a substantial change in American foreign policy.

1 / PRESIDENT MCKINLEY ASKS FOR INTERVENTION IN CUBA

President William McKinley (1843–1901), like his predecessor, Grover Cleveland, and the conservative American business community, initially opposed both imperialist expansion and intervention in Cuba. After the sinking of the Maine *in Havana Harbor, however, he yielded to the pressure of public opinion and the demands of political expediency. On April 11, 1898, he called on Congress to authorize an American effort to end the Cuban fighting and to free the island from Spanish rule. He did not foresee that his action would lead the United States to acquire colonies and to enter fully upon the stage of world politics.*

To the Congress of the United States:

Obedient to that precept of the Constitution which commands the President to give from time to time to the Congress information of the state of the Union and to recommend to their consideration such measures as he shall judge necessary and expedient, it becomes my duty to now address your body with

SOURCE: James D. Richardson (ed.), *A Compilation of the Messages and Papers of the Presidents, 1789–1897* (Washington, 1899), X, 139–50.

regard to the grave crisis that has arisen in the relations of the United States to Spain by reason of the warfare that for more than three years has raged in the neighboring island of Cuba.

I do so because of the intimate connection of the Cuban question with the state of our own Union and the grave relation the course which it is now incumbent upon the nation to adopt must needs bear to the traditional policy of our Government if it is to accord with the precepts laid down by the founders of the Republic and religiously observed by succeeding Administrations to the present day.

The present revolution is but the successor of other similar insurrections which have occurred in Cuba against the dominion of Spain, extending over a period of nearly half a century, each of which during its progress has subjected the United States to great effort and expense in enforcing its neutrality laws, caused enormous losses to American trade and commerce, caused irritation, annoyance, and disturbance among our citizens, and, by the exercise of cruel, barbarous, and uncivilized practices of warfare, shocked the sensibilities and offended the humane sympathies of our people.

Since the present revolution began, in February, 1895, this country has seen the fertile domain at our threshold ravaged by fire and sword in the course of a struggle unequaled in the history of the island and rarely paralleled as to the numbers of the combatants and the bitterness of the contest by any revolution of modern times where a dependent people striving to be free have been opposed by the power of the sovereign state.

Our people have beheld a once prosperous community reduced to comparative want, its lucrative commerce virtually paralyzed, its exceptional productiveness diminished, its fields laid waste, its mills in ruins, and its people perishing by tens of thousands from hunger and destitution. We have found ourselves constrained, in the observance of that strict neutrality which our laws enjoin and which the law of nations commands, to police our own waters and watch our own seaports in prevention of any unlawful act in aid of the Cubans.

Our trade has suffered, the capital invested by our citizens in Cuba has been largely lost, and the temper and forbearance of our people have been so sorely tried as to beget a perilous unrest among our own citizens, which has inevitably found its expression from time to time in the National Legislature, so that issues wholly external to our own body politic engross attention and stand in the way of that close devotion to domestic advancement that becomes a self-contained commonwealth whose primal maxim has been the avoidance of all foreign entanglements. All this must needs awaken, and has, indeed, aroused, the utmost concern on the part of this Government, as well during my predecessor's term as in my own. . . .

The war in Cuba is of such a nature that, short of subjugation or extermination, a final military victory for either side seems impracticable. The alternative lies in the physical exhaustion of the one or the other party, or perhaps of both—a condition which in effect ended the ten years' war by the truce of Zanjon. The prospect of such a protraction and conclusion of the present strife is a contingency hardly to be contemplated with equanimity by the civilized world, and least of all by the United States, affected and injured as we are, deeply and intimately, by its very existence. . . .

The forcible intervention of the United States as a neutral to stop the war, according to the large dictates of humanity and following many historical precedents where neighboring states have interfered to check the hopeless sacrifices of life by internecine conflicts beyond their borders, is justifiable on rational grounds. It involves, however, hostile constraint upon both the parties to the contest, as well to enforce a truce as to guide the eventual settlement.

The grounds for such intervention may be briefly summarized as follows:

First. In the cause of humanity and to put an end to the barbarities, bloodshed, starvation, and horrible miseries now existing there, and which the parties to the conflict are either unable or unwilling to stop or mitigate. It is no answer to say this is all in another country, belonging to another nation, and is therefore none of our business. It is specially our duty, for it is right at our door.

Second. We owe it to our citizens in Cuba to afford them that

protection and indemnity for life and property which no government there can or will afford, and to that end to terminate the
conditions that deprive them of legal protection.

Third. The right to intervene may be justified by the very
serious injury to the commerce, trade, and business of our people
and by the wanton destruction of property and devastation of the
island.

Fourth, and which is of the utmost importance. The present
condition of affairs in Cuba is a constant menace to our peace
and entails upon this Government an enormous expense. With
such a conflict waged for years in an island so near us and with
which our people have such trade and business relations; when
the lives and liberty of our citizens are in constant danger and
their property destroyed and themselves ruined; where our trading vessels are liable to be seized at our very door by war ships
of a foreign nation; the expeditions of filibustering that we are
powerless to prevent altogether, and the irritating questions and
entanglements thus arising—all these and others that I need not
mention, with the resulting strained relations, are a constant
menace to our peace and compel us to keep on a semi war foot-
ing with a nation with which we are at peace.

These elements of danger and disorder already pointed out
have been strikingly illustrated by a tragic event which has
deeply and justly moved the American people. I have already
transmitted to Congress the report of the naval court of inquiry
on the destruction of the battle ship *Maine* in the harbor of
Havana during the night of the 15th of February. The destruction of that noble vessel has filled the national heart with in-
expressible horror. Two hundred and fifty-eight brave sailors
and marines and two officers of our Navy, reposing in the fan-
cied security of a friendly harbor, have been hurled to death,
grief and want brought to their homes and sorrow to the nation.

The naval court of inquiry, which, it is needless to say, commands the unqualified confidence of the Government, was unanimous in its conclusion that the destruction of the *Maine* was
caused by an exterior explosion—that of a submarine mine. It
did not assume to place the responsibility. That remains to be
fixed.

In any event, the destruction of the *Maine*, by whatever exterior cause, is a patent and impressive proof of a state of things in Cuba that is intolerable. That condition is thus shown to be such that the Spanish Government can not assure safety to a vessel of the American Navy in the harbor of Havana on a mission of peace, and rightfully there. . . .

The long trial has proved that the object for which Spain has waged the war can not be attained. The fire of insurrection may flame or may smolder with varying seasons, but it has not been and it is plain that it can not be extinguished by present methods. The only hope of relief and repose from a condition which can no longer be endured is the enforced pacification of Cuba. In the name of humanity, in the name of civilization, in behalf of endangered American interests which give us the right and the duty to speak and to act, the war in Cuba must stop.

In view of these facts and of these considerations I ask the Congress to authorize and empower the President to take measures to secure a full and final termination of hostilities between the Government of Spain and the people of Cuba, and to secure in the island the establishment of a stable government, capable of maintaining order and observing its international obligations, insuring peace and tranquillity and the security of its citizens as well as our own, and to use the military and naval forces of the United States as may be necessary for these purposes.

2 / CARL SCHURZ OUTLINES THE PERILS OF IMPERIALISM

Carl Schurz (1829–1906), a Civil War major general, former Minister to Spain, and Secretary of the Interior under Benjamin Harrison, took up the anti-imperialist cause in the early 1890's. He foresaw that the Spanish-American War would lead to the acquisition of colonies and in September 1898, while the war was still in progress, published his warning against such a step. Far more than the imperialists, Schurz realized that taking on the burdens of empire would drastically alter the traditional world role of the United States. His fear of shattering domestic effects was doubtless exaggerated.

But how if this war of humanity and disinterested benevolence be turned into a war of conquest? How if Cuba or any other of the conquered islands be kept by the United States as a permanent possession? . . . A little sober reflection will convince every thinking mind that the first step on our part in this new policy of conquest will be very apt to fill the minds of our southern neighbors with that vague dread of some great danger hanging over them which will turn them into secret or open enemies of the United States, capable of throwing themselves into anybody's arms for protection; and this will not at all be unlikely to encourage, among old-world Powers, schemes of encroachment upon the American continent which, on account of the former relations between the smaller American republics and the United States under the Monroe Doctrine, have so far not ven-

SOURCE: "Thoughts on American Imperialism," *Century Magazine,* LVI (1898), 781–88.

tured forth. This would be to the United States the beginning of incalculable troubles of a new sort. And then these very troubles arising from southern hostility, combining with the ambitious schemes of old-world Powers, would be used by our imperialists as additional proof of the necessity of further conquests, and of the building up of the grand American empire embracing not only all the conquests made in the Spanish war, but reaching down to the Isthmus of Panama, with the islands within reach, and strong enough to meet all those accumulating difficulties.

To do justice to the subject, we have to face this grand imperial conception in its full development; for when once fairly launched, this is the direction in which we shall drift. Imagine, then, the United States to cover that part of America here described, and, in addition, Hawaii, the Philippines and perhaps the Carolines and the Ladrones [Marianas], and what not,— immense territories inhabited by white people of Spanish descent, by Indians, negroes, mixed Spanish and Indians, mixed Spanish and negroes, Hawaiians, Hawaiian mixed blood, Spanish Filipinos, Malays, Tagals, various kinds of savages and half-savages, not to mention the Chinese and Japanese—at least twenty-five millions in all and all of them animated with the instincts, impulses and passions bred by the tropical sun; and all those people to become Americans!

Some of the most prominent imperialists, by the way, have been in a great flurry about a few thousand immigrants from Italy, Russia and Hungary, because their becoming part of the American people would depress American labor and lower the standards of American citizenship. Now they would take in Spanish-Americans, with all the mixtures of Indian and negro blood, and Malays and other unspeakable Asiatics, by the tens of millions! What will become of American labor and the standards of American citizenship then?

We are vexed by a very troublesome race problem in the United States now. That race problem is still unsolved, and it would be very sanguine to say that there is a satisfactory solution in near prospect. Cool-headed men think that we have enough of that. What will be the consequence if we indefinitely add to it by bringing under this Republican Government big lots of other incompatible races—races far more intractable, too, than those with which we have so far had to deal?

But more. Owing to the multiplicity of churches, sects and denominations, and to their being mixed together in every part of the country and their pretty well balancing one another, there have been so far hardly any very serious difficulties of a religious nature in the United States. But if the imperial policy prevails, and all those countries, with their populations, are annexed, there will be for the first time in the history of the Republic, large territories inhabited by many millions of people who, with few exceptions, all belong to one church, and who, if they become a political force, may cause conflicts of influences from which the American people have so far been happily exempt.

I mention these things in order to indicate some of the difficulties we have to meet in considering the question how such countries and populations are to be fitted into our system of government. It is hard to see how the Spanish-American republics which are to be annexed could in the long run be refused admission as States, having, nominally at least, been governing themselves for many years. The Spanish-American islands would soon follow. Ambitious partisans, looking out for party votes in Congress and in the Electoral College, would certainly contrive to lug them in. There would then be a large lot of Spanish-Americans in the Senate and in the House and among the Presidential electors—more than enough of them to hold, occasionally at least, the balance of power in making laws not only for themselves, but for the whole American people, and in giving the Republic its Presidents. There would be "the Spanish-American vote"—being occasionally the decisive vote—to be bargained with. Who will doubt that of all the so-called "foreign votes" this country has ever had, this would be by far the most dangerous? It is useless to hope that this population would gradually assimilate itself to the American people as they now are. It might assimilate itself under the influence of our northern climate, but not in the tropics. In the tropics the Anglo-Saxon race is in the long run more apt to assimilate itself to the Spanish-American than the Spanish-American to the Anglo-Saxon. This is common experience.

The admission as States of the Philippines, the Carolines and so on,—that is, the transformation of "the United States of America" into "the United States of America and Asia,"—would, I suppose, appear too monstrous to be seriously thought of even by the wildest imperialist. Those countries, with an aggregate of about ten million inhabitants, would have to be governed as subject provinces, with no expectation of their becoming self-governing States. This means government without the consent of the governed. It means taxation without representation. It means the very things against which the Declaration of Independence remonstrated, and against which the Fathers rose in revolution. It means that the American people would carry on over large subject populations a kind of rule against which their own government is the most solemn protest. It may be said that those countries and populations cannot be governed in any other way; but is not that the most conclusive reason why this Republic should not attempt to govern them at all?

Against such an attempt there are other reasons hardly less vital. No candid observer of current events in this Republic will deny that the exercise of more or less arbitrary rule over distant countries will be apt to produce most pernicious effects upon our public morals. The farther away those subject countries are from close public observation, the richer and more tempting their natural resources, the more unfit their populations for self-government and the more pronounced the race antagonisms, the more unrestrained will be the cupidity of the governing race, the less respect will there be for the rights and interests of the subject races and the more unscrupulous and rapacious the rule over them—and this in spite of laws for their protection which may be fair on their face and well intended in their meaning. There has been much complaint of the influence wielded in our Government by rich and powerful corporations such as the Sugar Trust. The more or less arbitrary control exercised by our Government over distant countries with great resources will inevitably stimulate the multiplication of speculative enterprises with much money behind them, subjecting the Government in all its branches to constant pressure and manipulation which cannot fail to produce a most baneful effect upon our politics. Of such things we have experience enough to warn us.

But the combinations formed for distant adventure will be the most dangerous of all. Never having enough, their greed constantly grasping for more, they will seek to drive this country into new enterprises of conquest. Opportunities will not be lacking when this Republic is once in the race for colonial acquisitions in which the European Powers are now engaged, and which keeps them incessantly increasing their expensive armaments. And the more such enterprises there are, the greater will be the danger of new wars, with all their demoralizing effects upon our democratic government. It is, therefore, not too much to say—indeed, it is rather stating the fact very mildly—that the governing of distant countries as subject provinces would result in a fearful increase of the elements of profligacy and corruption in our political life.

3 / SENATOR BEVERIDGE CALLS

AMERICA TO GREATNESS

Senator Albert J. Beveridge of Indiana (1862–1927) was the most eloquent spokesman for the American nationalist-imperialist school, which also included Henry Cabot Lodge and Theodore Roosevelt. In his celebrated speech in Congress on January 9, 1900, he urged annexation of the Philippines at least in part for economic reasons. The whole tenor of his remarks indicates, however, that an emotional acceptance of a sense of mission and a romantic vision of American greatness were more basic to his position than calculations of economic interest.

Mr. President, the times call for candor. The Philippines are ours forever, "territory belonging to the United States," as the Constitution calls them. And just beyond the Philippines are China's illimitable markets. We will not retreat from either. We will not repudiate our duty in the archipelago. We will not abandon our opportunity in the Orient. We will not renounce our part in the mission of our race, trustee, under God, of the civilization of the world. And we will move forward to our work, not howling out regrets like slaves whipped to their burdens, but with gratitude for a task worthy of our strength, and thanksgiving to Almighty God that He has marked us as His chosen people, henceforth to lead in the regeneration of the world.

This island empire is the last land left in all the oceans. If it should prove a mistake to abandon it, the blunder once made would be irretrievable. If it proves a mistake to hold it, the error can be corrected when we will. Every other progressive nation stands ready to relieve us.

But to hold it will be no mistake. Our largest trade henceforth must be with Asia. The Pacific is our ocean. More and more Europe will manufacture the most it needs, secure from its colonies the most it consumes. Where shall we turn for consumers of our surplus? Geography answers the question. China is our natural customer. She is nearer to us than to England, Germany, or Russia, the commercial powers of the present and the future. They have moved nearer to China by securing permanent bases on her borders. The Philippines give us a base at the door of all the East.

Lines of navigation from our ports to the Orient and Australia; from the Isthmian Canal to Asia; from all Oriental ports to Australia, converge at and separate from the Philippines. They are a self-supporting, dividend-paying fleet, permanently anchored at a spot selected by the strategy of Providence, commanding the Pacific. And the Pacific is the ocean of the commerce of the future. Most future wars will be conflicts for commerce. The power that rules the Pacific, therefore, is the power that rules

SOURCE: *Congressional Record,* 56th Cong., 1st sess. (1900), pp. 704-12.

the world. And, with the Philippines, that power is and will forever be the American Republic. . . .

But if they did not command China, India, the Orient, the whole Pacific for purposes of offense, defense, and trade, the Philippines are so valuable in themselves that we should hold them. . . .

. . . Spain's export and import trade, with the islands undeveloped, was $11,534,731 annually. Our trade with the islands developed will be $125,000,000 annually, for who believes that we can not do ten times as well as Spain? Consider their imperial dimensions. Luzon is larger and richer than New York, Pennsylvania, Illinois, or Ohio. Mindanao is larger and richer than all New England, exclusive of Maine. Manila, as a port of call and exchange, will, in the time of men now living, far surpass Liverpool. Behold the exhaustless markets they command. It is as if a half dozen of our States were set down between Oceania and the Orient, and those States themselves undeveloped and unspoiled of their primitive wealth and resources. . . .

Here, then, Senators, is the situation. Two years ago there was no land in all the world which we could occupy for any purpose. Our commerce was daily turning toward the Orient, and geography and trade developments made necessary our commercial empire over the Pacific. And in that ocean we had no commercial, naval, or military base. To-day we have one of the three great ocean possessions of the globe, located at the most commanding commercial, naval, and military points in the eastern seas, within hail of India, shoulder to shoulder with China, richer in its own resources than any equal body of land on the entire globe, and peopled by a race which civilization demands shall be improved. Shall we abandon it? That man little knows the common people of the Republic, little understands the instincts of our race, who thinks we will not hold it fast and hold it forever, administering just government by simplest methods. . . .

But, Senators, it would be better to abandon this combined garden and Gibraltar of the Pacific, and count our blood and treasure already spent a profitable loss, than to apply any academic arrangement of self-government to these children. They are not capable of self-government. How could they be? They are not a self-governing race. They are Orientals, Malays, instructed by Spaniards in the latter's worst estate.

They know nothing of practical government except as they have witnessed the weak, corrupt, cruel, and capricious rule of Spain. What magic will anyone employ to dissolve in their minds and characters those impressions of governors and governed which three centuries of misrule has created? What alchemy will change the oriental quality of their blood and set the self-governing currents of the American pouring through their Malay veins? How shall they, in the twinkling of an eye, be exalted to the heights of self-governing peoples which required a thousand years for us to reach, Anglo-Saxon though we are? . . .

Mr. President, self-government and internal development have been the dominant notes of our first century; administration and the development of other lands will be the dominant notes of our second century. And administration is as high and holy a function as self-government, just as the care of a trust estate is as sacred an obligation as the management of our own concerns. Cain was the first to violate the divine law of human society which makes of us our brother's keeper. And administration of good government is the first lesson in self-government, that exalted estate toward which all civilization tends.

Administration of good government is not denial of liberty. For what is liberty? It is not savagery. It is not the exercise of individual will. It is not dictatorship. It involves government, but not necessarily self-government. It means law. First of all, it is a common rule of action, applying equally to all within its limits. Liberty means protection of property and life without price, free speech without intimidation, justice without purchase or delay, government without favor or favorites. What will best give all this to the people of the Philippines—American administration, developing them gradually toward self-government, or self-government by a people before they know what self-government means? . . .

Mr. President, this question is deeper than any question of party politics; deeper than any question of the isolated policy of our country even; deeper even than any question of constitutional power. It is elemental. It is racial. God has not been preparing the English-speaking and Teutonic peoples for a thousand years for nothing but vain and idle self-contemplation and self-admiration. No! He has made us the master organizers of the world to establish system where chaos reigns. He has given us the spirit of progress to overwhelm the forces of reaction throughout the earth. He has made us adepts in government that we may administer government among savage and senile peoples. Were it not for such a force as this the world would relapse into barbarism and night. And of all our race He has marked the American people as His chosen nation to finally lead in the regeneration of the world. This is the divine mission of America, and it holds for us all the profit, all the glory, all the happiness possible to man. We are trustees of the world's progress, guardians of its righteous peace. The judgment of the Master is upon us: "Ye have been faithful over a few things; I will make you ruler over many things."

What shall history say of us? Shall it say that we renounced that holy trust, left the savage to his base condition, the wilderness to the reign of waste, deserted duty, abandoned glory, forgot our sordid profit even, because we feared our strength and read the charter of our powers with the doubter's eye and the quibbler's mind? Shall it say that, called by events to captain and command the proudest, ablest, purest race of history in history's noblest work, we declined that great commission? Our fathers would not have it so. No! They founded no paralytic government, incapable of the simplest acts of administration. They planted no sluggard people, passive while the world's work calls them. They established no reactionary nation. They unfurled no retreating flag.

That flag has never paused in its onward march. Who dares halt it now—now, when history's largest events are carrying it forward; now, when we are at last one people, strong enough for any task, great enough for any glory destiny can bestow?

4 / PRESIDENT THEODORE ROOSEVELT
EXTENDS THE MONROE DOCTRINE

As the first President faced with the problems raised by America's new world role, Theodore Roosevelt (1858–1919) acted energetically to safeguard United States interests in the Caribbean and the Far East. Yet, though he was willing to use force and the threat of force to achieve his objectives, he essentially regarded such intervention in world affairs as an emergency measure to be used in specific cases and not as a new and permanent American policy. His fourth and fifth annual messages to Congress, dated December 6, 1904, and December 5, 1905, show how little he expected American involvement in European rivalries, as well as his sanguine belief that the United States could protect its own interests with a minimum of financial or military expenditure.

We are in every way endeavoring to help on, with cordial good-will, every movement which will tend to bring us into more friendly relations with the rest of mankind. In pursuance of this policy I shall shortly lay before the Senate treaties of arbitration with all powers which are willing to enter into these treaties with us. It is not possible at this period of the world's development to agree to arbitrate all matters, but there are many matters of possible difference between us and other nations which can be thus arbitrated. Furthermore, at the request of the Inter-parliamentary Union, an eminent body composed of practical statesmen from all countries, I have asked the powers to join

SOURCE: *The Works of Theodore Roosevelt* (Memorial Edition; New York: Charles Scribner's Sons, 1925), XVII, 250–310, 315–400.

with this government in a second Hague conference, at which it is hoped that the work already so happily begun at The Hague may be carried some steps further toward completion. This carries out the desire expressed by the first Hague conference itself.

It is not true that the United States feels any land hunger or entertains any projects as regards the other nations of the western hemisphere save such as are for their welfare. All that this country desires is to see the neighboring countries stable, orderly, and prosperous. Any country whose people conduct themselves well can count upon our hearty friendship. If a nation shows that it knows how to act with reasonable efficiency and decency in social and political matters, if it keeps order and pays its obligations, it need fear no interference from the United States. Chronic wrong-doing, or an impotence which results in a general loosening of the ties of civilized society, may in America, as elsewhere, ultimately require intervention by some civilized nation, and in the western hemisphere the adherence of the United States to the Monroe Doctrine may force the United States, however reluctantly, in flagrant cases of such wrong-doing or impotence, to the exercise of an international police power. If every country washed by the Caribbean Sea would show the progress in stable and just civilization which with the aid of the Platt amendment Cuba has shown since our troops left the island, and which so many of the republics in both Americas are constantly and brilliantly showing, all question of interference by this nation with their affairs would be at an end. Our interests and those of our Southern neighbors are in reality identical. They have great natural riches, and if within their borders the reign of law and justice obtains, prosperity is sure to come to them. While they thus obey the primary laws of civilized society they may rest assured that they will be treated by us in a spirit of cordial and helpful sympathy. We would interfere with them only in the last resort, and then only if it became evident that their inability or unwillingness to do justice at home and abroad had violated the rights of the United States or had invited foreign aggression to the detriment of the entire body of American nations. . . .

In asserting the Monroe Doctrine, in taking such steps as we have taken in regard to Cuba, Venezuela, and Panama, and in endeavoring to circumscribe the theatre of war in the Far East, and to secure the open door in China, we have acted in our own interest as well as in the interest of humanity at large. There are, however, cases in which, while our own interests are not greatly involved, strong appeal is made to our sympathies. Ordinarily it is very much wiser and of more useful material betterment to concern ourselves here at home than with trying to better the condition of things in other nations. We have plenty of sins of our own to war against, and under ordinary circumstances we can do more for the general uplifting of humanity by striving with heart and soul to put a stop to civic corruption, to brutal lawlessness and violent race prejudices here at home than by passing resolutions about wrong-doing elsewhere. Nevertheless there are occasional crimes committed on so vast a scale and of such peculiar horror as to make us doubt whether it is not our manifest duty to endeavor at least to show our disapproval of the deed and our sympathy with those who have suffered by it. The cases must be extreme in which such a course is justifiable. There must be no effort made to remove the mote from our brother's eye if we refuse to remove the beam from our own. But in extreme cases action may be justifiable and proper. What form the action shall take must depend upon the circumstances of the case; that is, upon the degree of the atrocity and upon our power to remedy it. The cases in which we could interfere by force of arms as we interfered to put a stop to intolerable conditions in Cuba are necessarily very few. Yet it is not to be expected that a people like ours, which in spite of certain very obvious shortcomings, nevertheless as a whole shows by its consistent practice its belief in the principles of civil and religious liberty and of orderly freedom, a people among whom even the worst crime, like the crime of lynching, is never more than sporadic, so that individuals and not classes are molested in their fundamental rights—it is inevitable that such a nation should desire eagerly to give expression to its horror on an occasion like that of the massacre of the Jews in Kishenef, or when it witnesses such systematic and long-extended cruelty and oppression as the cruelty and oppression of which the Armenians have been the victims, and which have won for them the indignant pity of the civilized world. . . .

. . . . .

Santo Domingo, in her turn, has now made an appeal to us to help her, and not only every principle of wisdom but every generous instinct within us bids us respond to the appeal. It is not of the slightest consequence whether we grant the aid needed by Santo Domingo as an incident to the wise development of the Monroe Doctrine or because we regard the case of Santo Domingo as standing wholly by itself, and to be treated as such, and not on general principles or with any reference to the Monroe Doctrine. The important point is to give the needed aid, and the case is certainly sufficiently peculiar to deserve to be judged purely on its own merits. The conditions in Santo Domingo have for a number of years grown from bad to worse until a year ago all society was on the verge of dissolution. Fortunately, just at this time a ruler sprang up in Santo Domingo, who, with his colleagues, saw the dangers threatening their country and appealed to the friendship of the only great and powerful neighbor who possessed the power, and as they hoped also the will to help them. There was imminent danger of foreign intervention. The previous ruler of Santo Domingo had recklessly incurred debts, and owing to her internal disorders she had ceased to be able to provide means of paying the debts. The patience of her foreign creditors had become exhausted, and at least two foreign nations were on the point of intervention, and were only prevented from intervening by the unofficial assurance of this government that it would itself strive to help Santo Domingo in her hour of need. In the case of one of these nations, only the actual opening of negotiations to this end by our government prevented the seizure of territory in Santo Domingo by a European power. Of the debts incurred some were just, while some were not of a character which really renders it obligatory on or proper for Santo Domingo to pay them in full. But she could not pay any of them unless some stability was assured her government and people.

Accordingly, the Executive Department of our government

negotiated a treaty under which we are to try to help the Dominican people to straighten out their finances. This treaty is pending before the Senate. In the meantime a temporary arrangement has been made which will last until the Senate has had time to take action upon the treaty. Under this arrangement the Dominican Government has appointed Americans to all the important positions in the customs service, and they are seeing to the honest collection of the revenues, turning over forty-five per cent to the government for running expenses and putting the other fifty-five per cent into a safe depository for equitable division in case the treaty shall be ratified, among the various creditors, whether European or American. . . .

. . . Under the proposed treaty the independence of the island is scrupulously respected, the danger of violation of the Monroe Doctrine by the intervention of foreign powers vanishes, and the interference of our government is minimized, so that we shall only act in conjunction with the Santo Domingo authorities to secure the proper administration of the customs, and therefore to secure the payment of just debts and to secure the Dominican Government against demands for unjust debts. The proposed method will give the people of Santo Domingo the same chance to move onward and upward which we have already given to the people of Cuba.

5 / PRESIDENT TAFT ADVOCATES DOLLAR DIPLOMACY

*Like his predecessor, President William Howard Taft
(1857–1930) saw America's foreign policy role as
limited essentially to the Far East and the Caribbean.
Less confident of the efficacy of military intervention,
the dire results of which he had observed in the
Philippines, Taft placed his faith in spreading
American influence through capital investment. In
his last annual message to Congress, dated December 3,
1912, he optimistically and unrealistically declared
this policy to have been successful.*

The diplomacy of the present administration has sought to
respond to modern ideas of commercial intercourse. This policy
has been characterized as substituting dollars for bullets. It is
one that appeals alike to idealistic humanitarian sentiments, to
the dictates of sound policy and strategy, and to legitimate commercial aims. It is an effort frankly directed to the increase of
American trade upon the axiomatic principle that the Government of the United States shall extend all proper support to
every legitimate and beneficial American enterprise abroad. How
great have been the results of this diplomacy, coupled with the
maximum and minimum provision of the tariff law, will be seen
by some consideration of the wonderful increase in the export
trade of the United States. Because modern diplomacy is commercial, there has been a disposition in some quarters to attribute
to it none but materialistic aims. How strikingly erroneous is such

SOURCE: *Papers Relating to the Foreign Relations of the United States,
1912* (Washington: Government Printing Office, 1919), pp. vii–xxvii.

an impression may be seen from a study of the results by which the diplomacy of the United States can be judged.

In the field of work toward the ideals of peace this Government negotiated, but to my regret was unable to consummate, two arbitration treaties which set the highest mark of the aspiration of nations toward the substitution of arbitration and reason for war in the settlement of international disputes. Through the efforts of American diplomacy several wars have been prevented or ended. I refer to the successful tripartite mediation of the Argentine Republic, Brazil, and the United States between Peru and Ecuador; the bringing of the boundary dispute between Panama and Costa Rica to peaceful arbitration; the staying of warlike preparations when Haiti and the Dominican Republic were on the verge of hostilities; the stopping of a war in Nicaragua; the halting of internecine strife in Honduras. The Government of the United States was thanked for its influence toward the restoration of amicable relations between the Argentine Republic and Bolivia. The diplomacy of the United States is active in seeking to assuage the remaining ill-feeling between this country and the Republic of Colombia. In the recent civil war in China the United States successfully joined with the other interested powers in urging an early cessation of hostilities. An agreement has been reached between the Governments of Chile and Peru whereby the celebrated Tacna-Arica dispute, which has so long embittered international relations on the west coast of South America, has at last been adjusted. Simultaneously came the news that the boundary dispute between Peru and Ecuador had entered upon a stage of amicable settlement. The position of the United States in reference to the Tacna-Arica dispute between Chile and Peru has been one of nonintervention, but one of friendly influence and pacific counsel throughout the period during which the dispute in question has been the subject of interchange of views between this Government and the two Governments immediately concerned. In the general easing of international tension on the west coast of South America the tripartite mediation, to which I have referred, has been a most potent and beneficent factor.

In China the policy of encouraging financial investment to

enable that country to help itself has had the result of giving new life and practical application to the open-door policy. The consistent purpose of the present administration has been to encourage the use of American capital in the development of China by the promotion of those essential reforms to which China is pledged by treaties with the United States and other powers. The hypothecation to foreign bankers in connection with certain industrial enterprises, such as the Hukuang railways, of the national revenues upon which these reforms depended, led the Department of State early in the administration to demand for American citizens participation in such enterprises, in order that the United States might have equal rights and an equal voice in all questions pertaining to the disposition of the public revenues concerned. The same policy of promoting international accord among the powers having similar treaty rights as ourselves in the matters of reform, which could not be put into practical effect without the common consent of all, was likewise adopted in the case of the loan desired by China for the reform of its currency. The principle of international cooperation in matters of common interest upon which our policy had already been based in all of the above instances has admittedly been a great factor in that concert of the powers which has been so happily conspicuous during the perilous period of transition through which the great Chinese nation has been passing.

In Central America the aim has been to help such countries as Nicaragua and Honduras to help themselves. They are the immediate beneficiaries. The national benefit to the United States is twofold. First, it is obvious that the Monroe doctrine is more vital in the neighborhood of the Panama Canal and the zone of the Caribbean than anywhere else. There, too, the maintenance of that doctrine falls most heavily upon the United States. It is therefore essential that the countries within that sphere shall be removed from the jeopardy involved by heavy foreign debt and chaotic national finances and from the ever-present danger of international complications due to disorder at home. Hence the United States has been glad to encourage and support American bankers who were willing to lend a helping hand to the financial rehabilitation of such countries because this financial rehabilitation and the protection of their customhouses from being the prey of would-be dictators would remove at one stroke the menace of foreign creditors and the menace of revolutionary disorder.

The second advantage to the United States is one affecting chiefly all the southern and Gulf ports and the business and industry of the South. The Republics of Central America and the Caribbean possess great natural wealth. They need only a measure of stability and the means of financial regeneration to enter upon an era of peace and prosperity, bringing profit and happiness to themselves and at the same time creating conditions sure to lead to a flourishing interchange of trade with this country. . . .

As illustrating the commercial benefits to the Nation derived from the new diplomacy and its effectiveness upon the material as well as the more ideal side, it may be remarked that through direct official efforts alone there have been obtained in the course of this administration, contracts from foreign Governments involving an expenditure of $50,000,000 in the factories of the United States. Consideration of this fact and some reflection upon the necessary effects of a scientific tariff system and a foreign service alert and equipped to cooperate with the business men of America carry the conviction that the gratifying increase in the export trade of this country is, in substantial amount, due to our improved governmental methods of protecting and stimulating it. . . .

Congress should fully realize the conditions which obtain in the world as we find ourselves at the threshold of our middle age as a Nation. We have emerged full grown as a peer in the great concourse of nations. We have passed through various formative periods. We have been self-centered in the struggle to develop our domestic resources and deal with our domestic questions. The Nation is now too mature to continue in its foreign relations those temporary expedients natural to a people to whom domestic affairs are the sole concern. In the past our diplomacy has often consisted, in normal times, in a mere assertion of the right to international existence. We are now in a larger relation with broader rights of our own and obligations to others than ourselves. A number of great guiding principles were laid down early in the history of this Government. The recent task of our diplomacy has been to adjust those principles as to the conditions of to-day, to develop their corollaries, to find practical applications of the old principles expanded to meet new situations. Thus are being evolved bases upon which can rest the superstructure of policies which must grow with the destined progress of this Nation. The successful conduct of our foreign relations demands a broad and a modern view. We can not meet new questions nor build for the future if we confine ourselves to outworn dogmas of the past and to the perspective appropriate at our emergence from colonial times and conditions. The opening of the Panama Canal will mark a new era in our international life and create new and world-wide conditions which, with their vast correlations and consequences, will obtain for hundreds of years to come. We must not wait for events to overtake us unawares. With continuity of purpose we must deal with the problems of our external relations by a diplomacy modern, resourceful, magnanimous, and fittingly expressive of the high ideals of a great nation.

PART II

The United States in a World at War, I

(1915-1919)

THE outbreak of war in Europe in July of 1914 auto-matically produced the traditional American response: a declara-tion of neutrality. The United States consequently sought to rely on an impartial defense of its rights as a neutral against encroach-ments by both groups of belligerents (Selection 6). There were those, however, who realized very quickly that for a major power to assume a pose of neutrality meant, in effect, abandoning both its interests and its principles. Theodore Roosevelt, for example, came to that conclusion by 1915 (Selection 7). Despite his great fears of the effects of war on the United States, Woodrow Wilson took a similar position early in 1917 (Selection 8).

Wilson's decision that nonintervention would, in the long run, be more harmful than intervention was challenged by those who saw going to war as an abandonment of traditional American policy unwarranted by world conditions (Selection 9) and who used the same arguments employed by the anti-imperialists two decades earlier. Yet it could also be argued that American entry into the war in order to defend its own interests and protect its principles did not violate the precepts of Washington and Jeffer-son. Unilaterally decided intervention did not necessarily mean either a permanent alliance or an undesirable entanglement. Many Americans supported entry into the war, therefore, with-out sanctioning a basic change in U.S. foreign policy.

Wilson's interest in the establishment of a supranational agency

41

for the settlement of international disputes raised a new problem for American policy makers, however. If entry into the war could be reconciled with traditional policies, membership in the League of Nations clearly could not. Wilson's defense of the League and his insistence on the necessity for American membership (Selection 10) could therefore be attacked with complete justification as requiring a major change in American foreign policy (Selection 11). The issue confronting the American people in 1919 was that of deciding whether such a change was desirable or necessary. Their initial decision was in the negative.

6 / SECRETARY OF STATE BRYAN
ADMONISHES THE BELLIGERENTS

William Jennings Bryan (1860–1925) regarded diplomacy solely as a means for the peaceful settlement of international disputes and spent most of his tenure as Secretary of State negotiating "cooling-off" treaties with some thirty-one countries. He was unalterably opposed to American involvement in the World War. When Great Britain unilaterally amended the accepted rules relating to contraband and blockade, Bryan merely lectured her on the rights of neutrals. When a German U-boat sank the British passenger liner Lusitania *and 128 Americans lost their lives, he expressed surprise and indignation but took no firm stand. Wilson's insistence on a second, stronger* Lusitania *note to Germany brought Bryan's resignation.*

You are instructed to deliver the following to His Majesty's Government in reply to your numbers 1795 and 1798 on March 15:

SOURCE: R. S. Baker and W. E. Dodd (eds.), *The Public Papers of Woodrow Wilson: The New Democracy* (New York, Harper and Bros., 1926), I, 289–96, 323–28. Reprinted with the permission of Harper & Row.

The Government of the United States has given careful consideration to the subjects treated in the British notes of March 13 and March 15, and to the British Order in Council of the latter date.

These communications contain matters of grave importance to neutral nations. They appear to menace their rights of trade and intercourse not only with belligerents but also with one another. They call for frank comment in order that misunderstandings may be avoided. The Government of the United States deems it its duty, therefore, speaking in the sincerest spirit of friendship, to make its own view and position with regard to them unmistakably clear.

The Order in Council of the 15th of March would constitute, were its provisions to be actually carried into effect as they stand, a practical assertion of unlimited belligerent rights over neutral commerce within the whole European area, and an almost unqualified denial of the sovereign rights of the nations now at peace. . . .

The Government of the United States is, of course, not oblivious to the great changes which have occurred in the conditions and means of naval warfare since the rules hitherto governing legal blockade were formulated. It might be ready to admit that the old form of "close" blockade with its cordon of ships in the immediate offing of the blockaded ports is no longer practicable in face of an enemy possessing the means and opportunity to make an effective defense by the use of submarines, mines, and air craft; but it can hardly be maintained that, whatever form of effective blockade may be made use of, it is impossible to conform at least to the spirit and principles of the established rules of war. . . .

The Government of the United States notes that in the Order in Council His Majesty's Government give as their reason for entering upon a course of action, which they are aware is without precedent in modern warfare, the necessity they conceive themselves to have been placed under to retaliate upon their enemies for measures of a similar nature which the latter have announced it their intention to adopt and which they have to some extent adopted; but the Government of the United States, recalling the principles upon which His Majesty's Government have hitherto been scrupulous to act, interprets this as merely a reason for certain extraordinary activities on the part of His Majesty's naval forces and not as an excuse for or prelude to any unlawful action. If the course pursued by the present enemies of Great Britain should prove to be in fact tainted by illegality and disregard of the principles of war sanctioned by enlightened nations, it can not be supposed, and this Government does not for a moment suppose, that His Majesty's Government would wish the same taint to attach to their own actions or would cite such illegal acts as in any sense or degree a justification for similar practices on their part in so far as they affect neutral rights. . . .

The possibilities of serious interruption of American trade under the Order in Council are so many, and the methods proposed are so unusual and seem liable to constitute so great an impediment and embarrassment to neutral commerce that the Government of the United States, if the Order in Council is strictly enforced, apprehends many interferences with its legitimate trade which will impose upon His Majesty's Government heavy responsibilities for acts of the British authorities clearly subversive of the rights of neutral nations on the high seas. It is, therefore, expected that His Majesty's Government, having considered these possibilities, will take the steps necessary to avoid them, and, in the event that they should unhappily occur, will be prepared to make full reparation for every act which under the rules of international law constitutes a violation of neutral rights.

As stated in its communication of October 22, 1914, "this Government will insist that the rights and duties of the United States and its citizens in the present war be defined by the existing rules of international law and the treaties of the United States, irrespective of the provisions of the Declaration of London, and that this Government reserves to itself the right to enter a protest or demand in each case in which those rights and duties so defined are violated or their free exercise interfered with, by the authorities of the British Government."

In conclusion you will reiterate to His Majesty's Government that this statement of the views of the Government of the United States is made in the most friendly spirit, and in accordance with the uniform candor which has characterized the relations of the two Governments in the past, and which has been in large measure the foundation of the peace and amity existing between the two nations without interruption for a century.

. . . . .

Please call on the Minister of Foreign Affairs and after reading to him this communication leave with him a copy.

In view of recent acts of the German authorities in violation of American rights on the high seas which culminated in the torpedoing and sinking of the British steamship *Lusitania* on May 7, 1915, by which over 100 American citizens lost their lives, it is clearly wise and desirable that the Government of the United States and the Imperial German Government should come to a clear and full understanding as to the grave situation which has resulted. . . .

Recalling the humane and enlightened attitude hitherto assumed by the Imperial German Government in matters of international right, and particularly with regard to the freedom of the seas; having learned to recognize the German views and the German influence in the field of international obligation as always engaged upon the side of justice and humanity; and having understood the instructions of the Imperial German Government to its naval commanders to be upon the same plane of humane action prescribed by the naval codes of other nations, the Government of the United States was loath to believe—it can not now bring itself to believe—that these acts, so absolutely contrary to the rules, the practices, and the spirit of modern warfare, could have the countenance or sanction of that great Government. . . .

The Government of the United States has been apprised that the Imperial German Government considered themselves to be obliged by the extraordinary circumstances of the present war and the measures adopted by their adversaries in seeking to cut Germany off from all commerce, to adopt methods of retaliation which go much beyond the ordinary methods of warfare at sea, in the proclamation of a war zone from which they have warned neutral ships to keep away. This Government has already taken occasion to inform the Imperial German Government that it cannot admit the adoption of such measures or such a warning of danger to operate as in any degree an abbreviation of the rights of American shipmasters or of American citizens bound on lawful errands as passengers on merchant ships of belligerent nationality; and that it must hold the Imperial German Government to a strict accountability for any infringement of those rights, intentional or incidental. . . .

The Government and people of the United States look to the Imperial German Government for just, prompt, and enlightened action in this vital matter with the greater confidence because the United States and Germany are bound together not only by special ties of friendship but also by the explicit stipulations of the treaty of 1828 between the United States and the Kingdom of Prussia.

Expressions of regret and offers of reparation in case of the destruction of neutral ships sunk by mistake, while they may satisfy international obligations, if no loss of life results, can not justify or excuse a practice, the natural and necessary effect of which is to subject neutral nations and neutral persons to new and immeasurable risks.

The Imperial German Government will not expect the Government of the United States to omit any word or any act necessary to the performance of its sacred duty of maintaining the rights of the United States and its citizens and of safeguarding their free exercise and enjoyment.

7 / FORMER PRESIDENT THEODORE ROOSEVELT DECRIES TIMID NEUTRALITY

To Roosevelt, Bryan's attitude appeared to be both cowardly and unrealistic. In his book America and the World War *he argued vigorously that the United States must defend its rights at whatever cost and, by standing up for principles of justice, lay the foundation for international order. It was the first clear assertion that America's world-wide interests required firm action in any and all international crises and that the earlier policy of aloofness in world affairs had outlived its usefulness.*

. . . We are a people different from, but akin to, all the nations of Europe. We should feel a real friendship for each of the contesting powers and a real desire to work so as to secure justice for each. This cannot be done by preserving a tame and spiritless neutrality which treats good and evil on precisely the same basis. Such a neutrality never has enabled and never will enable any nation to do a great work for righteousness. Our true course should be to judge each nation on its conduct, unhesitatingly to antagonize every nation that does ill as regards the point on which it does ill, and equally without hesitation to act, as cool-headed and yet generous wisdom may dictate, so as disinterestedly to further the welfare of all. . . .

SOURCE: *The Works of Theodore Roosevelt: America and the World War* (Memorial Edition; New York: Charles Scribner's Sons, 1925), XX, 191–216. Reprinted with permission of Charles Scribner's Sons. Copyright 1915 Charles Scribner's Sons; copyright 1943 Edith K. Carow Roosevelt.

I feel in the strongest way that we should have interfered, at least to the extent of the most emphatic diplomatic protest and at the very outset—and then by whatever further action was necessary—in regard to the violation of the neutrality of Belgium; for this act was the earliest and the most important and, in its consequences, the most ruinous of all the violations and offenses against treaties committed by any combatant during the war. But it was not the only one. The Japanese and English forces not long after violated Chinese neturality in attacking Kiao-Chau. It has been alleged and not denied that the British ship *Highflyer* sunk the *Kaiser Wilhelm der Grosse* in neutral Spanish waters, this being also a violation of The Hague conventions; and on October 10th the German Government issued an official protest about alleged violations of the Geneva convention by the Frerch. Furthermore, the methods employed in strewing portions of the seas with floating mines have been such as to warrant the most careful investigation by any neutral nations which treat neutrailty pacts and Hague conventions as other than merely dead letters. Not a few offenses have been committed against our own people.

If, instead of observing a timid and spiritless neutrality, we had lived up to our obligations by taking action in all of these cases without regard to which power it was that was alleged to have done wrong, we would have followed the only course that would both have told for world righteousness and have served our own self-respect. The course actually followed by Messrs. Wilson, Bryan, and Daniels has been to permit our own power for self-defense steadily to diminish while at the same time refusing to do what we were solemnly bound to do in order to protest against wrong and to render some kind of aid to weak nations that had been wronged. . . .

Our business is to create the beginnings of international order out of the world of nations as these nations actually exist. We do not have to deal with a world of pacifists and therefore we must proceed on the assumption that treaties will never acquire sanctity until nations are ready to seal them with their blood. We are not striving for peace in heaven. That is not our affair. What we were bidden to strive for is "peace on earth and good-will toward men." To fulfil this injunction it is necessary to treat the earth as it is and men as they are, as an indispensable pre-requisite to making the earth a better place in which to live and men better fit to live in it. It is inexcusable moral culpability on our part to pretend to carry out this injunction in such fashion as to nullify it; and this we do if we make believe that the earth is what it is not and if our professions of bringing good-will toward men are in actual practice shown to be empty shams. Peace con-gresses, peace parades, the appointment and celebration of days of prayer for peace, and the like, which result merely in giving the participants the feeling that they have accomplished some-thing and are therefore to be excused from hard, practical work for righteousness, are empty shams. Treaties such as the recent all-inclusive arbitration treaties are worse than empty shams and convict us as a nation of moral culpability when our representa-tives sign them at the same time that they refuse to risk any-thing to make good the signatures we have already affixed to The Hague conventions. . . .

. . . Pacifists claim that we have acted so as to preserve the good-will of Europe and to exercise a guiding influence in the settlement of the war. This is an idea which appeals to the thoughtless, for it gratifies our desire to keep out of trouble and also our vanity by the hope that we shall do great things with small difficulty. It may or may not be that the settlement will finally be made by a peace congress in which the President of the United States will hold titular position of headship. But under conditions as they are now the real importance of the President in such a peace congress will be comparable to the real importance of the drum-major when he walks at the head of a regiment. Small boys regard the drum-major as much more important than the regimental commander; and the pacifist grown-ups who applaud peace congresses sometimes show as regards the drum-majors of these congresses the same touching lack of insight which small boys show toward real drum-majors. As a matter of fact, if the United States enters such a congress with nothing but a record of comfortable neutrality or tame acquiescence in violated Hague conventions, plus an array of vague treaties with no relation to actual facts, it will be allowed to fill the position of international drum-major and of nothing more; and even this position it will be allowed to fill only so long as it suits the convenience of the men who have done the actual fighting. . . .

Peace in Europe will be made by the warring nations. They and they alone will in fact determine the terms of settlement. The United States may be used as a convenient means of getting together; but that is all. If the nations of Europe desire peace and our assistance in securing it, it will be because they have fought as long as they will or can. It will not be because they regard us as having set a spiritual example to them by sitting idle, uttering cheap platitudes, and picking up their trade, while they have poured out their blood like water in support of the ideals in which, with all their hearts and souls, they believe. For us to assume superior virtue in the face of the war-worn nations of the Old World will not make us more acceptable as mediators among them. Such self-consciousness on our part will not impress the nations who have sacrificed and are sacrificing all that is dearest to them in the world, for the things that they believe to be the noblest in the world. The storm that is raging in Europe at this moment is terrible and evil; but it is also grand and noble. Untried men who live at ease will do well to remember that there is a certain sublimity even in Milton's defeated arch-angel, but none whatever in the spirits who kept neutral, who remained at peace, and dared side neither with hell nor with heaven. They will also do well to remember that when heroes have battled together, and have wrought good and evil, and when the time has come out of the contest to get all the good possible and to prevent as far as possible the evil from being made permanent, they will not be influenced much by the theory that soft and short-sighted outsiders have put themselves in better condition to stop war abroad by making themselves defenseless at home.

8 / PRESIDENT WILSON SEEKS
A WORLD SAFE FOR DEMOCRACY

Though he was basically a domestic reformer with little experience or interest in foreign policy and though he greatly feared the effect that mobilization for war would have on the United States, President Wilson (1856–1924) became convinced of the need for American intervention early in 1917. After all his efforts to secure a negotiated peace had failed, Wilson concluded that American interests would be threatened by a German victory and that the United States could not be an effective force in shaping the postwar world unless it appeared at the peace table in the role of a belligerent. On April 2, 1917, he appeared before Congress to ask for a declaration of war.

When I addressed the Congress on the twenty-sixth of February last I thought that it would suffice to assert our neutral rights with arms, our right to use the seas against unlawful interference, our right to keep our people safe against unlawful violence. But armed neutrality, it now appears, is impracticable. Because submarines are in effect outlaws when used as the German submarines have been used against merchant shipping, it is impossible to defend ships against their attacks as the law of nations has assumed that merchantmen would defend themselves against privateers or cruisers, visible craft giving chase upon the open sea. It is common prudence in such circumstances, grim necessity indeed, to endeavour to destroy them before they have shown their own intention. They must be dealt with upon sight, if dealt with at all. The German Government

SOURCE: *Congressional Record*, 65th Cong., 1st sess. (1917), pp. 102–4.

denies the right of neutrals to use arms at all within the areas of the sea which it has proscribed, even in the defense of rights which no modern publicist has ever before questioned their right to defend. The intimation is conveyed that the armed guards which we have placed on our merchant ships will be treated as beyond the pale of law and subject to be dealt with as pirates would be. Armed neutrality is ineffectual enough at best; in such circumstances and in the face of such pretensions it is worse than ineffectual: it is likely only to produce what it was meant to prevent; it is practically certain to draw us into the war without either the rights or the effectiveness of belligerents. There is one choice we cannot make, we are incapable of making: we will not choose the path of submission and suffer the most sacred rights of our nation and our people to be ignored or violated. The wrongs against which we now array ourselves are no common wrongs; they cut to the very roots of human life.

With a profound sense of the solemn and even tragical character of the step I am taking and of the grave responsibilities which it involves, but in unhesitating obedience to what I deem my constitutional duty, I advise that the Congress declare the recent course of the Imperial German Government to be in fact nothing less than war against the government and people of the United States; that it formally accept the status of belligerent which has thus been thrust upon it; and that it take immediate steps not only to put the country in a more thorough state of defense but also to exert all its power and employ all its resources to bring the Government of the German Empire to terms and end the war.

What this will involve is clear. It will involve the utmost practicable cooperation in counsel and action with the governments now at war with Germany, and, as incident to that, the extension to those governments of the most liberal financial credits, in order that our resources may so far as possible be added to theirs. It will involve the organization and mobilization of all the material resources of the country to supply the materials of war and serve the incidental needs of the nation in the most abundant and yet the most economical and efficient way possible. It will involve the immediate full equipment of the navy in all respects but particularly in supplying it with the best means of dealing with the enemy's submarines. It will involve the immediate addition to the armed forces of the United States already provided for by law in case of war at least five hundred thousand men, who should, in my opinion, be chosen upon the principle of universal liability to service, and also the authorization of subsequent additional increments of equal force so soon as they may be needed and can be handled in training. It will involve also, of course, the granting of adequate credits to the Government, sustained, I hope, so far as they can equitably be sustained by the present generation, by well conceived taxation. . . .

While we do these things, these deeply momentous things, let us be very clear, and make very clear to all the world what our motives and our objects are. My own thought has not been driven from its habitual and normal course by the unhappy events of the last two months, and I do not believe that the thought of the nation has been altered or clouded by them. I have exactly the same things in mind now that I had in mind when I addressed the Senate on the twenty-second of January last; the same that I had in mind when I addressed the Congress on the third of February and on the twenty-sixth of February. Our object now, as then, is to vindicate the principles of peace and justice in the life of the world as against selfish and autocratic power and to set up amongst the really free and self-governed peoples of the world such a concert of purpose and of action as will henceforth ensure the observance of those principles. Neutrality is no longer feasible or desirable where the peace of the world is involved and the freedom of its peoples, and the menace to that peace and freedom lies in the existence of autocratic governments backed by organized force which is controlled wholly by their will, not by the will of their people. We have seen the last of neutrality in such circumstances. We are at the beginning of an age in which it will be insisted that the same standards of conduct and of responsibility for wrong done shall be observed among nations and their governments that are observed among the individual citizens of civilized states. . . .

One of the things that has served to convince us that the Prussian autocracy was not and could never be our friend is that from the very outset of the present war it has filled our unsuspecting communities and even our offices of government with spies and set criminal intrigues everywhere afoot against our national unity of counsel, our peace within and without, our industries and our commerce. Indeed it is now evident that its spies were here even before the war began; and it is unhappily not a matter of conjecture but a fact proved in our courts of justice that the intrigues which have more than once come perilously near to disturbing the peace and dislocating the industries of the country have been carried on at the instigation, with the support, and even under the personal direction of official agents of the Imperial Government accredited to the Government of the United States. Even in checking these things and trying to extirpate them we have sought to put the most generous interpretation possible upon them because we knew that their source lay, not in any hostile feeling or purpose of the German people towards us (who were, no doubt as ignorant of them as we ourselves were), but only in the selfish designs of a Government that did what it pleased and told its people nothing. But they have played their part in serving to convince us at last that that Government entertains no real friendship for us and means to act against our peace and security at its convenience. That it means to stir up enemies against us at our very doors the intercepted note to the German Minister at Mexico City is eloquent evidence.

We are accepting this challenge of hostile purpose because we know that in such a government, following such methods, we can never have a friend; and that in the presence of its organized power, always lying in wait to accomplish we know not what purpose, there can be no assured security for the democratic governments of the world. We are now about to accept gauge of battle with this natural foe to liberty and shall, if necessary, spend the whole force of the nation to check and nullify its pretensions and its power. We are glad, now that we see the facts with no veil of false pretence about them, to fight thus for the ultimate peace of the world and for the liberation of its peoples, the German peoples included: for the rights of nations great and small and the privilege of men everywhere to choose their way of life and of obedience. The world must be made safe for democracy. Its peace must be planted upon the tested foundations of political liberty. We have no selfish ends to serve. We desire no conquest, no dominion. We seek no indemnities for ourselves, no material compensation for the sacrifices we shall freely make. We are but one of the champions of the rights of mankind. We shall be satisfied when those rights have been made as secure as the faith and the freedom of nations can make them.

Just because we fight without rancour and without selfish object, seeking nothing for ourselves but what we shall wish to share with all free peoples, we shall, I feel confident, conduct our operations as belligerents without passion and ourselves observe with proud punctilio the principles of right and of fair play we profess to be fighting for. . . .

It is a distressing and oppressive duty, Gentlemen of the Congress, which I have performed in thus addressing you. There are, it may be, many months of fiery trial and sacrifice ahead of us. It is a fearful thing to lead this great peaceful people into war, into the most terrible and disastrous of all wars, civilization itself seeming to be in the balance. But the right is more precious than peace, and we shall fight for the things which we have always carried nearest our hearts,—for democracy, for the right of those who submit to authority to have a voice in their own governments, for the rights and liberties of small nations, for a universal dominion of right by such a concert of free peoples as shall bring peace and safety to all nations and make the world itself at last free. To such a task we can dedicate our lives and our fortunes, everything that we are and everything that we have, with the pride of those who know that the day has come when America is privileged to spend her blood and her might for the principles that gave her birth and happiness and the peace which she has treasured. God helping her, she can do no other.

9 / REPRESENTATIVE KITCHIN
WARNS AGAINST WAR

The Democratic majority leader in the House, Representative Claude Kitchin (1869–1923) of North Carolina, led the fight against a declaration of war. In his speech in Congress on April 5, 1917, he reiterated the traditional American policy of isolationism, pointing out that the United States had no direct interest in the war and could best contribute to the establishment of a peaceful world order by setting the example of remaining at peace.

Half the civilized world is now a slaughterhouse for human beings. This Nation is the last hope of peace on earth, good will toward men. I am unwilling for my country by statutory command to pull up the last anchor of peace in the world and extinguish during the long night of a world-wide war the only remaining star of hope for Christendom. I am unwilling by my vote to-day for this Nation to throw away the only remaining compass to which the world can look for guidance in the paths of right and truth, of justice and humanity, and to leave only force and blood to chart hereafter the path of mankind to tread.

By passage of this resolution we enter the war, and the universe becomes one vast drama of horrors and blood—one boundless stage upon which will play all the evil spirits of earth and hell. All the demons of inhumanity will be let loose for a rampage throughout the world. Whatever be the future, whatever be the rewards or penalties of this Nation's step, I shall always believe that we could and ought to have kept out of this war.

Great Britain every day, every hour, for two years has violated

SOURCE: *Congressional Record*, 65th Cong., 1st sess. (1917), pp. 332–33.

American rights on the seas. We have persistently protested. She has denied us not only entrance into the ports of the central powers but has closed to us by force the ports of neutrals. She has unlawfully seized our ships and our cargoes. She has rifled our mails. She has declared a war zone sufficiently large to cover all the ports of her enemy. She made the entire North Sea a military area—strewed it with hidden mines and told the neutral nations of the world to stay out or be blown up. We protested. No American ship was sunk, no American life was destroyed, because we submitted and did not go in. We kept out of war. We sacrificed no honor. We surrendered permanently no essential rights. We knew that these acts of Great Britain, though in plain violation of international law and of our rights on the seas, were not aimed at us. They were directed at her enemy. They were inspired by military necessity. Rather than plunge this country into war, we were willing to forego for the time our rights. I approved that course then; I approve it now.

Germany declares a war zone sufficiently large to cover the ports of her enemy. She infests it with submarines and warns the neutral world to stay out, though in plain violation of our rights and of international law. We know that these acts are aimed not directly at us but intended to injure and cripple her enemy, with which she is in a death struggle.

We refuse to yield; we refuse to forego our rights for the time. We insist upon going in.

In my judgment, we could keep out of the war with Germany as we kept out of the war with Great Britain, by keeping our ships and our citizens out of the war zone of Germany as we did out of the war zone of Great Britain. And we would sacrifice no more honor, surrender no more rights in the one case than in the other. Or we could resort to armed neutrality, which the President recently urged and for which I voted on March 1.

But we are told that Germany has destroyed American lives while Great Britain destroyed only property. Great Britain destroyed no American lives, because this Nation kept her ships and her citizens out of her war zone which she sowed with hidden mines.

But are we quite sure that the real reason for war with Germany is the destruction of lives as distinguished from property, that to avenge the killing of innocent Americans and to protect American lives war becomes a duty?

Mexican bandits raided American towns, shot to death sleeping men, women, and children in their own homes. We did not go to war to avenge these deaths. We sent an armed expedition into Mexico to hunt down and punish the bandits. Away out from the American border the soldiers of Carranza, of the Mexican Government, which we had recognized, met our soldiers, shot the American flag from the hands of an American soldier, shot down to the death our soldiers, and Carranza, instead of disavowing the dastardly act, definantly approved and ratified it. Yet we did not go to war to avenge the destruction of American lives and the insult and assault on the American flag. We were willing to forego our rights rather than plunge this country into war while half the world was in conflagration. I approved that course then; I approve it now.

Why can we not, why should we not, forego for the time being the violation of our rights by Germany, and do as we did with Great Britain, do as we did with Mexico, and thus save the universe from being wrapped in the flames of war.

I have hoped and prayed that God would forbid our country going into war with another for doing that which perhaps under the same circumstances we ourselves would do.

Are we quite sure that in a war with Germany or Japan, if our fleet was bottled up, helpless, and our ships of commerce had been swept from the seas, all our ports closed by the enemy's fleet, imports of fuel and food and clothing for our people and ammunition for our soldiers were denied, with our very life trembling in the balance, we would not, in the last struggle for existence, strike our enemy with the only weapon of the sea remaining, though in violation of international law? Would one contend that under the circumstances our submarine commanders should permit the landing at the ports of the enemy arms and ammunition with which to shoot down our brave American boys when they had it in their power to prevent it? Would we demand of our submarine commanders that they give the benefit of the doubt to questions of international law rather than to the safety of our country and the lives of our soldiers?

War upon the part of a nation is sometimes necessary and imperative. But here no invasion is threatened. Not a foot of our territory is demanded or coveted. No essential honor is required to be sacrificed. No fundamental right is asked to be permanently yielded or suspended. No national policy is contested. No part of our sovereignty is questioned. Here the overt act, ruthless and brutal though it be, is not aimed directly at us. The purpose of the proposed enemy is not our injury, either in property or life. The whole aim and purpose and effort are directed at a powerful enemy with which she is in a life and death struggle.

The causes for which we are now asked to declare war could have been given with equal—yea, greater—force 30 days or 10 days after the first step taken by the German Army in its march toward Paris. They existed then.

The House and the country should thoroughly understand that we are asked to declare war not to protect alone American lives and American rights on the high seas. We are to make the cause of Great Britain, France, and Russia, right or wrong, our cause. We are to make their quarrel, right or wrong, our quarrel. We are to help fight out, with all the resources in men, money, and credit of the Government and its people, a difference between the belligerents of Europe to which we were and are utter strangers. Nothing in that cause, nothing in that quarrel, has or does involve a moral or equitable or material interest in or obligation of our Government or our people.

10 / PRESIDENT WILSON PLEADS
FOR THE LEAGUE OF NATIONS

To Wilson, the major justification for American intervention had been the opportunity this step created for replacing international anarchy with international organization. The covenant of the League of Nations, which he had persuaded the Allies to include in the peace treaty, was to him, therefore, the keystone of his entire foreign policy. In a speech in Pueblo, Colorado, on October 6, 1919, when the treaty was already under bitter attack in the Senate, Wilson eloquently expressed his hopes for the future and warned that America's wartime sacrifices would have been in vain if the League of Nations were rejected. Wilson, in effect, urged a permanent commitment by the United States to the maintenance of world order.

Do not think of this treaty of peace as merely a settlement with Germany. It is that. It is a very severe settlement with Germany, but there is not anything in it that she did not earn. Indeed, she earned more than she can ever be able to pay for, and the punishment exacted of her is not a punishment greater than she can bear, and it is absolutely necessary in order that no other nation may ever plot such a thing against humanity and civilization. But the treaty is so much more than that. It is not merely a settlement with Germany; it is a readjustment of those great injustices which underlie the whole structure of European and Asiatic society. . . .

At the front of this great treaty is put the covenant of the league of nations. It will also be at the front of the Austrian

SOURCE: *Congressional Record*, 66th Cong., 1st sess. (1919), pp. 6424–27.

treaty and the Hungarian treaty and the Bulgarian treaty and the treaty with Turkey. Every one of them will contain the covenant of the league of nations, because you can not work any of them without the covenant of the league of nations. Unless you get the united, concerted purpose and power of the great Governments of the world behind this settlement, it will fall down like a house of cards. There is only one power to put behind the liberation of mankind, and that is the power of mankind. It is the power of the united moral forces of the world, and in the covenant of the league of nations the moral forces of the world are mobilized. . . . All the nations that have power that can be mobilized are going to be members of this league, including the United States. And what do they unite for? They enter into a solemn promise to one another that they will never use their power against one another for aggression; that they never will impair the territorial integrity of a neighbor; that they never will interfere with the political independence of a neighbor; that they will abide by the principle that great populations are entitled to determine their own destiny and that they will not interfere with that destiny; and that no matter what differences arise amongst them they will never resort to war without first having done one or the other of two things—either submitted the matter of controversy to arbitration, in which case they agree to abide by the result without question, or submitted it to the consideration of the council of the league of nations, laying before that council all the documents, all the facts, agreeing that the council can publish the documents and the facts to the whole world, agreeing that there shall be six months allowed for the mature consideration of those facts by the council, and agreeing that at the expiration of the six months, even if they are not then ready to accept the advice of the council with regard to the settlement of the dispute, they will still not go to war for another three months. In other words, they consent, no matter what happens, to submit every matter of difference between them to the judgment of mankind, and just so certainly as they do that, my fellow citizens, war will be in the far background, war will be pushed out of that foreground of terror in which it has kept the world for generation after generation, and men will know there will be a calm time of deliberate counsel. . . .

When you come to the heart of the covenant, my fellow citizens, you will find it in Article 10. . . . Article 10 provides that every member of the league covenants to respect and preserve the territorial integrity and existing political independence of every other member of the league as against external aggression. Not against internal disturbance. There was not a man at that table who did not admit the sacredness of the right of self-determination, the sacredness of the right of any body of people to say that they would not continue to live under the Government they were then living under, and under article 11 of the covenant they are given a place to say whether they will live under it or not. For following article 10 is article 11, which makes it the right of any member of the league at any time to call attention to anything, anywhere, that is likely to disturb the peace of the world or the good understanding between nations upon which the peace of the world depends. . . .

But you will say, "What is the second sentence of article 10? That is what gives very disturbing thoughts." The second sentence is that the council of the league shall advise what steps, if any, are necessary to carry out the guaranty of the first sentence, namely, that the members will respect and preserve the territorial integrity and political independence of the other members. I do not know any other meaning for the word "advise" except "advise." The council advises, and it can not advise without the vote of the United States. . . .

. . . The covenant in another portion guarantees to the members the independent control of their domestic questions. There is not a leg for these gentlemen to stand on when they say that the interests of the United States are not safeguarded in the very points where we are most sensitive. You do not need to be told again that the covenant expressly says that nothing in this covenant shall be construed as affecting the validity of the Monroe doctrine, for example. You could not be more explicit than that. And every point of interest is covered, partly for one very interesting reason. This is not the first time that the Foreign Relations Committee of the Senate of the United States has read and considered this covenant. I brought it to this country in March last in a tentative, provisional form, in practically the form that it now has, with the exception of certain additions which I shall mention immediately. I asked the Foreign Relations Committees of both Houses to come to the White House and we spent a long evening in the frankest discussion of every portion that they wished to discuss. They made certain specific suggestions as to what should be contained in this document when it was to be revised. I carried those suggestions to Paris, and every one of them was adopted. What more could I have done? What more could have been obtained? The very matters upon which these gentlemen were most concerned were, the right of withdrawal, which is now expressly stated; the safeguarding of the Monroe doctrine, which is now accomplished; the exclusion from action by the league of domestic questions, which is now accomplished. All along the line, every suggestion of the United States was adopted after the covenant had been drawn up in its first form and had been published for the criticism of the world. There is a very true sense in which I can say this is a tested American document.

I am dwelling upon these points, my fellow citizens, in spite of the fact that I dare say to most of you they are perfectly well known, because in order to meet the present situation we have got to know what we are dealing with. We are not dealing with the kind of document which this is represented by some gentlemen to be; and inasmuch as we are dealing with a document simon-pure in respect of the very principles we have professed and lived up to, we have got to do one or other of two things— we have got to adopt it or reject it. There is no middle course. You can not go in on a special-privilege basis of your own. I take it that you are too proud to ask to be exempted from responsibilities which the other members of the league will carry. We go in upon equal terms or we do not go in at all; and if we do not go in, my fellow citizens, think of the tragedy of that result—the only sufficient guaranty to the peace of the world withheld! Ourselves drawn apart with that dangerous pride which means that we shall be ready to take care of ourselves, and that means that we shall maintain great standing armies and an irresistible navy; that means we shall have the organization of a military nation; that means we shall have a general staff, with the kind of power that the general staff of Germany had, to mobilize this great manhood of the Nation when it pleases, all the energy of our young men drawn into the thought and preparation for war. What of our pledges to the men that lie dead in France? We said that they went over there, not to prove the prowess of America or her readiness for another war but to see to it that there never was such a war again. . . .

. . . I wish some men in public life who are now opposing the settlement . . . could feel the moral obligation that rests upon us not to go back on those boys, but to see the thing through, to see it through to the end and make good their redemption of the world. For nothing less depends upon this decision, nothing less than the liberation and salvation of the world.

11 / SENATOR LODGE VOICES

HIS RESERVATIONS

The permanence of the commitment proposed by Wilson was objected to by the opponents of the treaty, led by Senator Henry Cabot Lodge (1850–1924) of Massachusetts. Lodge had favored going to war because he believed specific American interests to have been at stake. Membership in the League of Nations, however, seemed to him to involve a curtailment of American sovereignty and a clear departure from the traditional nonentanglement policy laid down by Washington and Jefferson. In his speech in the Senate on August 12, 1919, he insisted that the League, far from contributing to world peace, would lead America into eternal wars.

. . . Turn to the preamble of the covenant of the league of nations now before us, which states the object of the league. It is formed "in order to promote international cooperation and to achieve international peace and security by the acceptance of obligations not to resort to war, by the prescription of open, just, and honorable relations between nations, by the firm establishment of the understandings of international laws as the actual rule of conduct among governments, and by the maintenance of justice and a scrupulous respect for all treaty obligations in the dealings of organized peoples with one another."

No one would contest the loftiness or the benevolence of these purposes. Brave words, indeed! They do not differ essentially from the preamble of the treaty of Paris, from which sprang the Holy Alliance. But the covenant of this league contains a provision which I do not find in the treaty of Paris, and which is as follows:

The assembly may deal at its meetings with any matter within the sphere of action of the league or affecting the peace of the world.

. . . No revolutionary movement, no internal conflict, of any magnitude can fail to affect the peace of the world. The French Revolution, which was wholly internal at the beginning, affected the peace of the world to such an extent that it brought on a world war which lasted some 25 years. Can anyone say that our Civil War did not affect the peace of the world? At this very moment, who would deny that the condition of Russia, with internal conflicts raging in all parts of that great Empire, does not affect the peace of the world and therefore come properly within the jurisdiction of the league? "Any matter affecting the peace of the world" is a very broad statement which could be made to justify almost any interference on the part of the league with the internal affairs of other countries. . . . If Europe desires such an alliance or league with a power of this kind, so be it. . . . But I object in the strongest possible way to having the United States agree, directly or indirectly, to be controlled by a league which may at any time, and perfectly lawfully and in

SOURCE: *Congressional Record*, 66th Cong., 1st sess. (1919), pp. 3778–84.

accordance with the terms of the covenant, be drawn in to deal with internal conflicts in other countries, no matter what those conflicts may be. We should never permit the United States to be involved in any internal conflict in another country, except by the will of her people expressed through the Congress which represents them.

With regard to wars of external aggression on a member of the league, the case is perfectly clear. There can be no genuine dispute whatever about the meaning of the first clause of article 10. . . . Each nation for itself promises to respect and preserve as against external aggression the boundaries and the political independence of every member of the league. . . .

If China should rise up and attack Japan in an effort to undo the great wrong of the cession of the control of Shantung to that power, we should be bound under the terms of article 10 to sustain Japan against China, and a guaranty of that sort is never invoked except when the question has passed beyond the stage of negotiation and has become a question for the application of force. I do not like the prospect. It shall not come into existence by any vote of mine.

Article 11 carries this danger still further, for it says:

Any war or threat of war, whether immediately affecting any of the members of the league or not, is hereby declared a matter of concern to the whole league and the league shall take any action that shall be deemed wise and effectual to safeguard the peace of nations.

"Any war or threat of war" means both external aggression and internal disturbance, as I have already pointed out in dealing with article 3. "Any action" covers military action, because it covers action of any sort or kind. . . .

. . . We are told that of course nothing will be done in the way of warlike acts without the assent of Congress. If that is true let us say so in the covenant. But as it stands there is no doubt whatever in my mind that American troops and American ships may be ordered to any part of the world by nations other than the United States, and that is a proposition to which I for one can never assent. It must be made perfectly clear that no American soldiers, not even a corporal's guard, that no American sailors, not even the crew of a submarine, can ever be engaged in war or ordered anywhere except by the constitutional authorities of the United States. . . . This is a point upon which no doubt can be permitted. American soldiers and American sailors have never failed the country when the country called upon them. They went in their hundreds of thousands into the war just closed. They went to die for the great cause of freedom and of civilization. . . . They overrode all obstacles and all shortcomings on the part of the administration or of Congress and gave to their country a great place in the great victory. It was the first time we had been called upon to rescue the civilized world. Did we fail? On the contrary, we succeeded, succeeded largely and nobly, and we did it without any command from any league of nations. When the emergency came we met it, and we were able to meet it because we had built up on this continent the greatest and most powerful Nation in the world, built it up under our own policies, in our own way, and one great element of our strength was the fact that we had held aloof and had not thrust ourselves into European quarrels; that we had no selfish interest to serve. We made great sacrifices. We have done splendid work. I believe that we do not require to be told by foreign nations when we shall do work which freedom and civilization require. I think we can move to victory much better under our own command than under the command of others. Let us unite with the world to promote the peaceable settlement of all international disputes. Let us try to develop international law. Let us associate ourselves with the other nations for these purposes. But let us retain in our own hands and in our own control the lives of the youth of the land. Let no American be sent into battle except by the constituted authorities of his own country and by the will of the people of the United States.

Those of us, Mr. President, who are either wholly opposed to the league, or who are trying to preserve the independence and the safety of the United States by changing the terms of the league and who are endeavoring to make the league, if we are to be a member of it, less certain to promote war instead of peace have been reproached with selfishness in our outlook and with a desire to keep our country in a state of isolation. So far as the question of isolation goes, it is impossible to isolate the United States. I well remember the time, 20 years ago, when eminent Senators and other distinguished gentlemen who were opposing the Philippines and shrieking about imperialism sneered at the statement made by some of us, that the United States had become a world power. I think no one now would question that the Spanish war marked the entrance of the United States into world affairs to a degree which had never obtained before. It was both an inevitable and an irrevocable step, and our entrance into the war with Germany certainly showed once and for all that the United States was not unmindful of its world responsibilities. We may set aside all this empty talk about isolation. Nobody expects to isolate the United States or to make it a hermit Nation, which is a sheer absurdity. But there is a wide difference between taking a suitable part and bearing a due responsibility in world affairs and plunging the United States into every controversy and conflict on the face of the globe. By meddling in all the differences which may arise among any portion or fragment of humankind we simply fritter away our influence and injure ourselves to no good purpose. We shall be of far more value to the world and its peace by occupying, so far as possible, the situation which we have occupied for the last 20 years and by adhering to the policy of Washington and Hamilton, of Jefferson and Monroe, under which we have risen to our present greatness and prosperity.

PART III

Between Isolation and Commitment

(1921–1937)

THE First World War increased both America's importance and America's reluctance to play an active role in world affairs. When some of the treaties resulting from the Washington Conference of 1921 implied a firm commitment to uphold the status quo in the Pacific, Congress was quick to add a disclaimer (Selection 12). With isolation impossible and commitment deemed undesirable, the American secretaries of state were forced to walk a narrow and poorly defined path throughout the 1920's. Charles Evans Hughes, for example, tried to continue the policies of Roosevelt and Taft by concentrating on the Caribbean and the Far East and avoiding involvement in European affairs (Selection 13).

As the twenties came to a close, however, it was obvious that a high degree of interdependence had developed among all nations and that the United States could ignore this interdependence only at its own peril. Yet even Hoover, who clearly recognized this, was not prepared to make the fundamental change in American foreign policy which this recognition seemed to demand (Selection 14).

With the advent of the Depression and the renewed gathering of war clouds in Europe and Asia, the notion that this interdependence was harmful to the United States and could and should be eliminated was once more expressed with vigor. The isolationists of the 1930's insisted on absolute independence for the United States in the foreign affairs area and made avoidance of war and its concomitant entanglements the primary goal of American policy (Selection 15).

President Roosevelt concentrated almost exclusively on domestic affairs until 1936. By the end of 1937, however, he began to make at least a tentative move toward awakening the American people to the dangers that threatened from abroad and toward urging this country to take positive steps to stop aggression and to prevent a general war (Selection 16). What he expressed was, at the time, still a minority viewpoint.

12 / THE UNITED STATES UPHOLDS
THE STATUS QUO IN ASIA

The ambiguous role assumed by the United States after its refusal to join the League of Nations is illustrated by the Four-Power and Nine-Power treaties produced by the Washington Conference of 1921. On the one hand, this country recognized its interest in world peace in general and in the Far East in particular by agreeing with other powers to uphold the status quo and to consult with them to plan joint actions whenever the status quo was threatened. On the other hand, Congress was quick to stipulate that such a commitment would not require armed intervention.

The United States of America, the British Empire, France and Japan,

SOURCE: *Treaties, Conventions, International Acts, Protocols and Agreements between the United States of America and Other Powers, 1776–1937* (Washington: Government Printing Office, 1910–1938), III, 3094–99, 3120–24.

With a view to the preservation of the general peace and the maintenance of their rights in relation to their insular possessions and insular dominions in the region of the Pacific Ocean,

Have determined to conclude a Treaty to this effect and . . . have agreed as follows:

I

The High Contracting Parties agree as between themselves to respect their rights in relation to their insular possessions and insular dominions in the region of the Pacific Ocean.

If there should develop between any of the High Contracting Parties a controversy arising out of any Pacific question and involving their said rights which is not satisfactorily settled by diplomacy and is likely to affect the harmonious accord now happily subsisting between them, they shall invite the other High Contracting Parties to a joint conference to which the whole subject will be referred for consideration and adjustment.

II

If the said rights are threatened by the aggressive action of any other Power, the High Contracting Parties shall communicate with one another fully and frankly in order to arrive at an understanding as to the most efficient measures to be taken, jointly or separately, to meet the exigencies of the particular situation.

III

This Treaty shall remain in force for ten years from the time it shall take effect, and after the expiration of said period it shall continue to be in force subject to the right of any of the High Contracting Parties to terminate it upon twelve months' notice.

. . . . .

In signing the Treaty this day between The United States of America, The British Empire, France and Japan, it is declared to be the understanding and intent of the Signatory Powers:

1. That the Treaty shall apply to the Mandated Islands in the Pacific Ocean; provided, however, that the making of the Treaty shall not be deemed to be an assent on the part of The United States of America to the mandates and shall not preclude agreements between The United States of America and the Mandatory Powers respectively in relation to the mandated islands.

2. That the controversies to which the second paragraph of Article I refers shall not be taken to embrace questions which according to principles of international law lie exclusively within the domestic jurisdiction of the respective Powers.

Resolved (*two-thirds of the Senators present concurring therein*), That the Senate advise and consent to the ratification of Executive N, Sixty-seventh Congress, second session, a treaty between the United States, the British Empire, France, and Japan relating to their insular possessions and insular dominions in the Pacific Ocean, concluded at Washington, December 13, 1921, subject to the following reservation and understanding, which is hereby made a part and condition of this resolution of ratification:

The United States understands that under the statement in the preamble or under the terms of this treaty there is no commitment to armed force, no alliance, no obligation to join in any defense.

⌣ ⌣ ⌣

The United States of America, Belgium, the British Empire, China, France, Italy, Japan, the Netherlands and Portugal:

Desiring to adopt a policy designed to stabilize conditions in the Far East, to safeguard the rights and interests of China, and to promote intercourse between China and the other Powers upon the basis of equality of opportunity;

Have resolved to conclude a treaty for that purpose and . . . have agreed as follows:

ARTICLE I

The Contracting Powers, other than China, agree:

(1) To respect the sovereignty, the independence, and the territorial and administrative integrity of China;

(2) To provide the fullest and most unembarrassed opportunity to China to develop and maintain for herself an effective and stable government;

(3) To use their influence for the purpose of effectually establishing and maintaining the principle of equal opportunity for the commerce and industry of all nations throughout the territory of China;

(4) To refrain from taking advantage of conditions in China in order to seek special rights or privileges which would abridge the rights of subjects or citizens of friendly States, and from countenancing action inimical to the security of such States.

Article II

The Contracting Powers agree not to enter into any treaty, agreement, arrangement, or understanding, either with one another, or, individually or collectively, with any Power or Powers, which would infringe or impair the principles stated in Article I.

Article III

With a view to applying more effectually the principles of the Open Door or equality of opportunity in China for the trade and industry of all nations, the Contracting Powers, other than China, agree that they will not seek, nor support their respective nationals in seeking:

(a) any arrangement which might purport to establish in favour of their interests any general superiority of rights with respect to commercial or economic development in any designated region of China;

(b) any such monopoly or preference as would deprive the nationals of any other Power of the right of undertaking any legitimate trade or industry in China, or of participating with the Chinese Government, or with any local authority, in any category of public enterprise, or which by reason of its scope, duration or geographical extent is calculated to frustrate the practical application of the principle of equal opportunity.

It is understood that the foregoing stipulations of this Article are not to be so construed as to prohibit the acquisition of such properties or rights as may be necessary to the conduct of a particular commercial, industrial, or financial undertaking or to the encouragement of invention and research.

China undertakes to be guided by the principles stated in the foregoing stipulations of this Article in dealing with applications for economic rights and privileges from Governments and nationals of all foreign countries, whether parties to the present Treaty or not.

Article IV

The Contracting Powers agree not to support any agreements by their respective nationals with each other designed to create Spheres of Influence or to provide for the enjoyment of mutually exclusive opportunities in designated parts of Chinese territory.

Article V

China agrees that, throughout the whole of the railways in China, she will not exercise or permit unfair discrimination of any kind. In particular there shall be no discrimination whatever, direct or indirect; in respect of charges or of facilities on the ground of the nationality of passengers or the countries from which or to which they are proceeding, or the origin or ownership of goods or the country from which or to which they are consigned, or the nationality or ownership of the ship or other means of conveying such passengers or goods before or after their transport on the Chinese Railways.

The Contracting Powers, other than China, assume a corresponding obligation in respect of any of the aforesaid railways over which they or their nationals are in a position to exercise any control in virtue of any concession, special agreement or otherwise.

Article VI

The Contracting Powers, other than China, agree fully to respect China's rights as a neutral in time of war to which China is not a party; and China declares that when she is a neutral she will observe the obligations of neutrality.

ARTICLE VII

The Contracting Powers agree that, whenever a situation arises which in the opinion of any one of them involves the application of the stipulations of the present Treaty, and renders desirable discussion of such application, there shall be full and frank communication between the Contracting Powers concerned.

ARTICLE VIII

Powers not signatory to the present Treaty, which have Governments recognized by the Signatory Powers and which have treaty relations with China, shall be invited to adhere to the present Treaty. To this end the Government of the United States will make the necessary communications to nonsignatory Powers and will inform the Contracting Powers of the replies received. Adherence by any Power shall become effective on receipt of notice thereof by the Government of the United States.

13 / SECRETARY OF STATE HUGHES URGES COOPERATION WITHOUT COMMITMENT

*Although Secretary of State Charles Evans Hughes's (1862–
1948) concern for world problems was demonstrated
by his call for the Washington Conference of
1921, both this action and the speech he delivered
on November 30, 1923, reveal that his major preoccupation
was still with the Caribbean and the Far East.
His determination to retain an independent position
with respect to European rivalries and his firm rejection
of any and all alliances indicate his basic adherence
to nineteenth-century American foreign policy principles.*

. . . We fought the Spanish War to put an end to an intolerable
nuisance at our very door, and to establish and make secure
the independence of Cuba, not to override it. And as a consequence of victory in that war we acquired distant possessions,
but not with the purpose of making these a basis for encroaching
upon the territory or interfering with the political independence
of the peoples of the eastern nations. In safeguarding the integrity of China, in securing equality of commercial opportunity,
in endeavoring to forestall efforts at exploitation and aggression,
in seeking to remove suspicion and allay apprehensions, and in
enlarging through assured tranquillity the opportunities of peaceful commerce, we have been pursuing under different conditions
the same aims of independence, security, and peace which determined the declaration of Monroe.

With respect to Europe, our policy has continued to be in

SOURCE: Charles Evans Hughes, *The Pathway to Peace* (New York: Harper
and Bros., 1925), pp. 142–63. Reprinted with permission of Harper &
Row.

the phrase of Jefferson: "Peace, commerce, and honest friendship with all nations, entangling alliances with none." We entered the Great War, not violating our tradition, for the cause of liberty itself was at stake. We have emerged from the war with the same general aims that we had before we went in. Though victors, we have sought neither territory nor general reparations. Our people have borne their own burdens and in large part we are bearing the burdens of others. We are not seeking to dictate to Europe or to deprive anyone of rights. But we do desire peace and economic recuperation in Europe. . . .

The bitter controversy which followed the war showed with what tenacity we still hold to the principle of not meddling in the political strife of Europe. It is true that the spread of democratic ideas and the resulting change in governments have removed the danger of organized effort to extend to this continent the European "political system" of 100 years ago. But Europe still has "a set of primary interests" which are not ours. As Washington said: "She must be engaged in political controversies the causes of which are essentially foreign to our concern." Unity in war did not avail to change the divergent national aims and policies in peace. It is not that our interests may not be affected injuriously by such controversies. That was true in the days of Washington, Jefferson, and Monroe; indeed the effect of changes and developments is that we are far better able to bear such injuries today than we were then, as is sufficiently illustrated by our sufferings during the Napoleonic Wars. But it was, despite such injuries, the abiding conviction that we had better bear these ills than suffer the greater evils which would follow the sacrifice of our independent position. We still hold to that view. . . .

. . . We are still opposed to alliances. We refuse to commit ourselves in advance with respect to the employment of the power of the United States in unknown contingencies. We reserve our judgment to act upon occasion as our sense of duty permits. We are opposed to discrimination against our nationals. We ask fair and equal opportunities in mandated territories as they were acquired by the Allies through our aid. We desire to co-operate according to our historic policy in the peaceful settlement of international disputes which embraces the policy of judicial settlement of such questions as are justicable. It is our purpose to co-operate in those varied humanitarian efforts which aim to minimize or prevent those evils which can be met adequately only by community of action. For example, we are at this moment leading in the effort to put a stop to the abuse of narcotic drugs. We strongly support, as our recent action has shown, international conferences where the conditions are such that they afford an instrumentality for the adjustment of differences and the formulation of useful conventions. We seek to aid in the reëstablishment of sound economic conditions. In short, our co-operation as an independent state in the furtherance of the aims of peace and justice has always been and still is a distinctive feature of our policy. . . .

. . . Our affirmative policies relating to our own conduct in relation to other American States, and not merely our policy with respect to the conduct of non-American powers, should be clearly envisaged. Those affirmative policies, while distinct from the mere principle of exclusion, set forth in the Monroe doctrine, are not inconsistent with that doctrine but rather constitute its fitting complement.

First, we recognize the equality of the American republics, their equal rights under the law of nations. . . .

Second, it follows that it is a part of our policy to respect the territorial integrity of the Latin-American republics. We have no policy of aggression; we do not support aggression by others; we are opposed to aggression by any one of the Latin-American republics upon any other. . . .

Third, states have duties as well as rights. Every state on being received into the family of nations accepts the obligations which are the essential conditions of international intercourse. Among these obligations is the duty of each state to respect the rights of citizens of other states which have been acquired within its jurisdiction in accordance with its laws. A confiscatory policy strikes not only at the interests of particular individuals but at the foundations of international intercourse, for it is only on the basis of the security of property validly possessed under the laws existing at the time of its acquisition that the conduct of activities in helpful co-operation is possible. Each state may have its code of laws in accordance with its conception of domestic policy, but rights acquired under its laws by citizens of another state it is under an international obligation appropriately to recognize. It is the policy of the United States to support these fundamental principles.

Fourth, it is the policy of this government to make available its friendly assistance to promote stability in those of our sister republics which are especially afflicted with disturbed conditions involving their own peace and that of their neighbors. It is the desire of the United States to render this assistance by methods that are welcomed and which are consistent with the general policies above stated. . . .

In promoting stability we do not threaten independence but seek to conserve it. We are not aiming at control but endeavoring to establish self-control. We are not seeking to add to our territory or to impose our rule upon other peoples.

Fifth, the United States aims to facilitate the peaceful settlement of difficulties between the governments in this hemisphere. . . .

Sixth, in seeking to promote peace, as well as to aid in the reduction of unproductive expenditures, this government has sought to encourage the making of agreements for the limitation of armament. . . .

Seventh, the policies which have been described are not to secure peace as an end in itself, but to make available the opportunities of peace; that is, to open the way to a mutually helpful co-operation. This is the object of the Pan American conferences. These will be increasingly helpful as they become more and more practical. The object is to create the opportunity for friendly contact, to develop a better appreciation of mutual interests and to find particular methods by which beneficial intercourse can be aided. This bears directly upon the facilitation of exchanges, the protection of health, the promotion of education and commerce and the developing of all the necessary agencies for disseminating information and for improving means of communication. With peace assured and apprehensions allayed, it will inevitably be found that there is less diversity of interest than had been supposed and that there is an ever-widening opportunity for working together for the common good.

Eighth, it should also be observed that in our commercial relations the United States is seeking unconditional most-favored-nation treatment in customs matters. . . .

Ninth, we have certain special policies of the highest importance to the United States.

We have established a waterway between the Atlantic and Pacific oceans—the Panama Canal. Apart from obvious commercial considerations, the adequate protection of this canal—its complete immunity from any adverse control—is essential to our peace and security. We intend in all circumstances to safeguard the Panama Canal. We could not afford to take any different position with respect to any other waterway that may be built between the Atlantic and the Pacific oceans. Disturbances in the Caribbean region are therefore of special interest to us not for the purpose of seeking control over others but of being assured that our own safety is free from menace.

With respect to Cuba, we have the special interests arising from our treaty and our part in the securing of her independence. It is our desire to see her independence not weakened but safeguarded and her stability and prosperity assured. Our friendly advice and aid are always available to that end. . . .

. . . We rejoice in the progress of our sister republics and at the enhanced prosperity which is at their call. The Monroe doctrine stands, as it has always stood, as an essential part of our defensive policy, but we are no less but rather more interested in the use of the opportunity which it created and has conserved. We desire no less than they themselves the independence, the peace and progress of all the American republics, and we seek to enjoy to the fullest extent possible the blessings bestowed by the spirit of confraternity, those mutual benefits which should result from our intimate association and our common political ideals.

14 / PRESIDENT HOOVER RECOGNIZES THE INTERDEPENDENCE OF NATIONS

*Despite his later isolationism, Herbert Hoover (1874–
1964) was more internationalist-minded than any of
his predecessors, with the exception of Wilson and
Roosevelt. In his Armistice Day speech in 1929 he
recognized that the United States was now too much
involved in world affairs to be able to afford to
ignore world problems. While rejecting participation
in the League of Nations, he nevertheless pointed out
the need for a more active foreign policy as a means of
preserving world peace.*

The world to-day is comparatively at peace. The outlook for
a peaceable future is more bright than for a half a century past.
Yet after all it is an armed peace. The men under arms including active reserves in the world are almost 30,000,000 in number,
or nearly 10,000,000 more than before the Great War. Due to
the Washington Arms Conference and the destruction of the
German Navy, the combatant ships in the world show some de-
crease since the war. But aircraft and other instruments of destruction are far more potent than they were even in the Great
War. There are fears, distrusts, and smouldering injuries among
nations which are the tinder of war. Nor does a single quarter
of a century during all the ages of human experience warrant
the assumption that war will not occur again.

Gloomy as this picture may be, yet we can say with truth
that the world is becoming more genuinely inclined to peace;

SOURCE: W. S. Myers (ed.), *State Papers and Other Public Writings of
Herbert Hoover* (Garden City: Doubleday, Doran & Co., 1934), I, 125–32.
Reprinted with permission of the Estate of Herbert Hoover.

that the forces of imperial domination and aggression, of fear and suspicion are dying down; that they are being replaced with the desire for security and peaceful development. The old objectives of tortuous diplomacy are being replaced with frank and open relations directed to peace. There is no more significant step in this progress than the solemn covenant that civilized nations have now entered, to renounce war and to settle disputes by pacific means. It is this realignment of the mind of the world that gives the hope of peace.

But peace is not a static thing. To maintain peace is as dynamic in its requirements as is the conduct of war. We can not say "Let there be peace" and go about other business. Nor are the methods by which peace is to be maintained and war prevented to be established by slogans or by abstract phrases or by academic theory. Progress toward peace can be attained only as a result of realistic practical daily conduct amongst nations. It can be the result only of a frank recognition of forces which may disturb peace. For instance, we must realize that our industrial life, our employment, our comfort, and our culture depend greatly upon our interchange of goods and ideas with other nations. We must realize that this interchange can not be carried on unless our citizens are flung into every quarter of the globe and the citizens of every nation are represented in our country.

We must realize that some of them will get into trouble somewhere. Certainly their troubles will multiply if other nations are at war. We have an obligation and every other nation has an obligation to see to the protection of their lives, and that justice is done to them so long as they comply with the laws of the countries in which they reside. From all these relationships frictions and controversies will arise daily.

By our undertaking under the Kellogg Pact, to use only pacific means to settle such controversies as these, we have again reaffirmed the doctrine enunciated by that far-sighted statesman, Mr. Elihu Root, in his famous declaration at Rio de Janeiro in 1907. At that time he announced that we would not use war or warlike means to enforce or collect upon private business contracts. It is our settled policy.

But there are other more deep-seated and more dangerous

forces which produce friction and controversy than these erup-
tions over the rights of citizens. We must realize that there are
many unsolved problems of boundaries between nations. There
are peoples aspiring to a greater measure of self-government.
There are the fears of invasion and domination bequeathed to
all humanity from its former wars. There are a host of age-old
controversies whose specters haunt the world, which at any time
may touch the springs of fear and ill will.

We must frankly accept the fact, therefore, that we and all
the nations of the world will be involved, for all future time,
in small or great controversies and frictions arising out of all of
these multiple causes. In these controversies lurks the subtle
danger that national temper at any moment may become a heat
and that emotion may rise to the flaming point. Therefore, peace
must be the result of unceasing endeavor.

I have said that recently we have covenanted with other
civilized nations not only to renounce war as an instrument of
national policy but also we have agreed that we shall settle all
controversies by pacific means. But the machinery for pacific
settlement of disputes among nations is, as yet, inadequate. We
need to strengthen our own provisions for it. Our State Department is the first of these means. It must be strengthened and
supported as the great arm of our government, dedicated to the
organization of peace. We need further to extend our treaties
with other countries providing methods for reference of controversies to conference, to inquiry as to fact, or to arbitration
or to judicial determination. We have need to define the rules
of conduct of nations and to formulate an authoritative system
of international law. We have need under proper reservations to
support the World Court in order that we may secure judicial
determination of certain types of controversies and build up
precedents which add to the body of international law. By these
agencies we relegate a thousand frictions to orderly processes
of settlement and by deliberation in action we prevent their
development into national inflammation.

We are also interested that other nations shall settle by pacific
means the controversies arising between them. From every selfish
point of view the preservation of peace among other nations is

of interest to the United States. In such wars we are in constant danger of entanglement because of interference with the widespread activities of our citizens. But of far more importance than this, our ideals and our hopes are for the progress of justice through the entire world. We desire to see all humanity relieved of the hideous blight of war and of the cruelties and injustices that lead to war. We are interested in all methods that can be devised to assure the settlement of all controversies between nations.

There are today two roads to that end. The European nations have, by the covenant to the League of Nations, agreed that if nations fail to settle their differences peaceably then force should be applied by other nations to compel them to be reasonable. We have refused to travel this road. We are confident that at least in the Western Hemisphere public opinion will suffice to check violence. This is the road we propose to travel. What we urgently need in this direction is a further development of methods for reference of unsettled controversies to joint inquiry by the parties assisted by friendly nations, in order that action may be stayed and that the aggressor may be subjected to the searchlight of public opinion. . . .

The colossal power of the United States overshadows scores of freedom-loving nations. Their defense against us is a moral defense. To give to them confidence that with the high moral sense of the American people this defense is more powerful than all armies or navies, is a sacred duty which lies upon us.

It has been my cherished hope to organize positively the foreign relations of the United States on this high foundation and to do it in reality, not simply in diplomatic phases. The establishment of that relationship is vastly more important than the mere settlement of the details of any of our chronic international problems. In such pure air and in that alone can both sides with frankness and candor present their points of view and either find just formulas for settlement, or, alternatively, agree to disagree until time finds a solution. We have in recent years heard a vast chatter of enmity and criticism both within and without our borders where there is no real enmity and no conflict of vital interest and no unsolvable controversy.

It is a homely parallel but equally true that relations between nations are much like relations between individuals. Questions which arise between friends are settled as the passing incidents of a day. The very same questions between men who distrust and suspect each other may lead to enmity and conflict.

It was in this endeavor that I visited the Presidents of the South American Republics. That is why I welcomed the visit of the Prime Minister of Great Britain to the United States.

All these men have talked of their problems in a spirit charged with the gravest responsibility, not only for our own relations but for the peace and safety of the world. We have thought out loud together as men can not think in diplomatic notes. We made no commitments. We drove no discussion to final conclusion. We explored the areas of possible constructive action and possible controversy. We examined the pitfalls of international relations frankly and openly. With this wider understanding of mutual difficulties and aspirations we can each in our own sphere better contribute to broaden good will, to assist those forces which make for peace in the world, to curb those forces which make for distrust.

15 / SENATOR BORAH ATTACKS
INTERNATIONALISM

*The same factors which led Hoover to an optimistic
conclusion in 1929 proved the failure of
internationalism to Senator William E. Borah (1865–
1940) of Idaho. As chairman of the Foreign Relations
Committee from 1924 to 1931 he had been an enthusiastic
supporter of the Kellogg-Briand Pact and a strong
advocate of American recognition of the Soviet Union.
In his speech before the Council on Foreign Relations
on January 8, 1934, he reiterated his basic isolationism,
however, and insisted that the world had not changed
sufficiently to warrant abandonment of traditional
American policies.*

In respect to international matters, the world has not changed,
the Orient has not changed, Europe has not changed. The nations were never so heavily armed in peace times as in the
fifteenth year after the signing of the armistice. Nearly $5,000,-
000,000 are annually extorted from impoverished peoples in
preparation for another war. National frontiers in many instances
are in effect battlefronts. The issues between certain leading
powers are as inexplicable and irreconcilable as they were before
the conflict began. The old system of the balance of power again
dominates the European Continent. Diplomatic moves bend to
its delusive assurances. The Corridor, the city of Danzig, Upper
Silesia, the problem of the minorities, Manchuria in the Orient,
the vindictive judgments of the peace treaties, the inequality of
nations, now the cornerstone of international law in Europe, all
these problems, truculent and inexorable, serve to keep Europe

SOURCE: *Congressional Record,* 73d Cong., 2d sess. (1939), 315–17.

armed and vigilant, and to warn us again and again that the reign of internationalism has not yet arrived. They are European problems arising out of conditions centuries old. The outside world cannot reach them. To make an attempt to do so would ignite the powder mine.

The answer to nationalism, it is insisted, is the nearness of all peoples by reason of modern invention and improved methods of transportation. Europe is now at our door, it is claimed, and Asia just around the corner. We therefore cannot be indifferent to their problems. We must have a part in all that concerns them, nearness makes their affairs our affairs. This matter of nearness seems to play strange pranks sometimes. It has certainly run counter to the expectations of many in the last twenty years, although we might have been well advised, since it had been doing the same things in crowded Europe for a thousand years. Nearness has not begotten there a common interest or a common purpose or even friendly relations. It has not mellowed the individuality of nations or fostered and strengthened the spirit of cooperation. It has not induced the belief that because of nearness there should be less of the national spirit. It has not put an end to war or rendered it less likely to occur. . . .

Another revolution, therefore, has failed. It had to fail. It could not escape the living past. It did not weigh sufficiently the inertia of human nature, it underestimated the strength of those ancient prejudices and fears, as well as those ancient faiths and beliefs, the intellectual and moral paths over which men and women had trodden for centuries. The fight against nationalism has lost. It was bound to lose. It was a fight against the strongest and noblest passion, outside of those which spring from man's relation to his God, that moves or controls the impulses of the human heart. Without it civilization would wane and utterly decay. Men would sink to the level of savages. Individuality in persons is the product of the most persistent and universal law of nature. It is woven of millions of subtle and tireless forces. No power can change this law or frustrate its operation. This is equally true of nations. Internationalism, if it means anything more than the friendly cooperation between separate, distinct, and wholly independent nations, rests upon a false foundation. And when undertaken, it will fail as in the name of progress and humanity it should fail. . . .

. . . I believe in the foreign policy which offers peace to all nations, trade and commerce with all nations, honest friendship with all nations, political commitments, express or implied, with none—the policy which not only in fact respects the rights and sovereignties of other states and nations without distinction of great and small, and particularly upon this Continent, but which would also refrain from words or acts that would seem to challenge those rights. Under the shelter and the inspiration of such a foreign policy I would foster and strengthen that brand of Americanism which believes in the worth, the efficiency, and grandeur of constitutional democracy, in the vigilant preservation of the personal liberty and the individual privileges of the citizen, realizing that our institutions and the whole vast scheme of democratic government depend upon our ability here on this western continent to harmonize the rapacious economic forces of the modern world with the political freedom and economic rights of the individual. Thus, armed with a sense of justice toward other nations on the one hand and a sense of duty toward our own people on the other, this nation will remain at peace with all nations who want peace, and if there be those who do not, and will not, have peace, we under such circumstances need have no fear. . . .

This, it will be said, is isolation. It is not isolation, it is freedom of action. It is independence of judgment. It is not isolation, it is free government; there can be no such thing as free government if the people thereof are not free to remain aloof or to take part in foreign wars. People who have bartered away or surrendered their rights to remain neutral in war have surrendered their right to govern. In matters of trade and commerce we have never been isolationists and never will be. In matters of finance, unfortunately, we have not been isolationists, and probably never will be. When earthquake and famine, or whatever brings human suffering, visit any part of the human race, we have not been isolationists, and never will be. In all those matters and things in which a free and independent enlightened people may have a part, looking toward amity, toward peace, and the lessening of human suffering, we have never been isolationists, and never will be. But in all matters political, in all commitments of any nature or kind, which encroach in the slightest upon the free and unembarrassed action of our people, or which circumscribe their discretion and judgment, we have been free, we have been independent, we have been isolationists. And this, I trust, we shall ever be. If there be any truth established by the experience of nations, it is this: That to accommodate your foreign policies to the demands or in the interest of other nations at the peril of your own security, is to invite contempt, and it seldom fails to earn a more substantial punishment.

In recent years much has been said, especially from abroad, about the provincial American. Those who discuss this and kindred matters modestly pay tribute to their own worth by speaking of world vision and of a wider human sympathy. One need hardly linger to discuss the subject. Regardless of what may be said by those whose purposes are apparent, let us hold fast to those political principles and foreign policies which others call provincialism, but which we call Americanism. It has served us well. It fits in with our scheme of democracy. It has built a civilization whose capstone is personal liberty. It may have its faults, as what earthly scheme has not. But all the world will have to testify that in great emergencies, in sublime moments, when civilization hangs in the balance, it is wanting neither in sympathy nor in courage, and whatever faults it may possess are buried in the depth of a great unselfish and heroic purpose. It has no taste, no aptitude, for the hazardous enterprise of uncovering aggressors or chastising national renegades. Here in its God-ordained home between two oceans, watchful of its own interests and vigilant in the defense of its rights, it covets nothing of others save the peace and friendship of all. It does not, and it never has, shrunk from its duty to civilization. It will not disown any obligations which human liberty and human justice impose upon a free people. But it does propose, I venture to prophesy, to determine for itself when civilization is threatened, when there may be a breach of human rights and human liberty sufficient to warrant action, and it proposes also to determine for itself when to act and in what manner it shall discharge the obligations which time and circumstances impose.

16 / PRESIDENT FRANKLIN D. ROOSEVELT

REQUESTS A QUARANTINE

OF AGGRESSORS

President Franklin D. Roosevelt (1882–1945) had torpedoed the London Economic Conference of 1933, rejected the possibility of League membership for the United States, and acquiesced in the adoption of the Neutrality Acts. In his Chicago speech of October 5, 1937, however, he suggested that the United States join with other law-abiding nations to halt aggression and to preserve peace. His trial balloon was promptly shot down, and he did not press the issue for fear of antagonizing Congressional isolationists whose support he needed for enactment of his domestic program. Characteristically, it was the Japanese advance in the Far East which prompted the speech.

The political situation in the world, which of late has been growing progressively worse, is such as to cause grave concern and anxiety to all the peoples and nations who wish to live in peace and amity with their neighbors.

Some 15 years ago the hopes of mankind for a continuing era of international peace were raised to great heights when

SOURCE: *Papers Relating to the Foreign Relations of the United States: Japan, 1931–1941* (Washington: Government Printing Office, 1943), I, 379–83.

more than 60 nations solemnly pledged themselves not to resort to arms in furtherance of their national aims and policies. The high aspirations expressed in the Briand-Kellogg Peace Pact and the hopes for peace thus raised have of late given way to a haunting fear of calamity. The present reign of terror and international lawlessness began a few years ago.

It began through unjustified interference in the internal affairs of other nations or the invasion of alien territory in violation of treaties and has now reached a stage where the very foundations of civilization are seriously threatened. The landmarks and traditions which have marked the progress of civilization toward a condition of law, order, and justice are being wiped away.

Without a declaration of war and without warning or justification of any kind, civilians, including women and children, are being ruthlessly murdered with bombs from the air. In times of so-called peace ships are being attacked and sunk by submarines without cause or notice. Nations are fomenting and taking sides in civil warfare in nations that have never done them any harm. Nations claiming freedom for themselves deny it to others.

Innocent peoples and nations are being cruelly sacrificed to a greed for power and supremacy which is devoid of all sense of justice and humane consideration.

To paraphrase a recent author, "perhaps we foresee a time when men, exultant in the technique of homicide, will rage so hotly over the world that every precious thing will be in danger, every book and picture and harmony, every treasure garnered through two millenniums, the small, the delicate, the defenseless —all will be lost or wrecked or utterly destroyed."

If those things come to pass in other parts of the world let no one imagine that America will escape, that it may expect mercy, that this Western Hemisphere will not be attacked, and that it will continue tranquilly and peacefully to carry on the ethics and the arts of civilization.

If those days come "there will be no safety by arms, no help from authority, no answer in science. The storm will rage till every flower of culture is trampled and all human beings are leveled in a vast chaos."

If those days are not to come to pass—if we are to have a world in which we can breathe freely and live in amity without fear—the peace-loving nations must make a concerted effort to uphold laws and principles on which alone peace can rest secure.

The peace-loving nations must make a concerted effort in opposition to those violations of treaties and those ignorings of humane instincts which today are creating a state of international anarchy and instability from which there is no escape through mere isolation or neutrality.

Those who cherish their freedom and recognize and respect the equal right of their neighbors to be free and live in peace, must work together for the triumph of law and moral principles in order that peace, justice, and confidence may prevail in the world. There must be a return to a belief in the pledged word, in the value of a signed treaty. There must be recognition of the fact that national morality is as vital as private morality. . . .

There is a solidarity and interdependence about the modern world, both technically and morally, which makes it impossible for any nation completely to isolate itself from economic and political upheavals in the rest of the world, especially when such upheavals appear to be spreading and not declining. There can be no stability or peace either within nations or between nations except under laws and moral standards adhered to by all. International anarchy destroys every foundation for peace. It jeopardizes either the immediate or the future security of every nation, large or small. It is, therefore, a matter of vital interest and concern to the people of the United States that the sanctity of international treaties and the maintenance of international morality be restored.

The overwhelming majority of the peoples and nations of the world today want to live in peace. They seek the removal of barriers against trade. They want to exert themselves in industry, in agriculture, and in business, that they may increase their wealth through the production of wealth-producing goods rather than striving to produce military planes and bombs and machine guns and cannon for the destruction of human lives and useful property.

In those nations of the world which seem to be piling armament on armament for purposes of aggression, and those other nations which fear acts of aggression against them and their security, a very high proportion of their national income is being spent directly for armaments. It runs from 30 to as high as 50 percent.

The proportion that we in the United States spend is far less —11 or 12 percent.

How happy we are that the circumstances of the moment permit us to put our money into bridges and boulevards, dams and reforestation, the conservation of our soil, and many other kinds of useful works rather than into huge standing armies and vast supplies of implements of war.

I am compelled and you are compelled, nevertheless, to look ahead. The peace, the freedom, and the security of 90 percent of the population of the world is being jeopardized by the remaining 10 percent, who are threatening a breakdown of all international order and law. Surely the 90 percent who want to live in peace under law and in accordance with moral standards that have received almost universal acceptance through the centuries, can and must find some way to make their will prevail.

The situation is definitely of universal concern. The questions involved relate not merely to violations of specific provisions of particular treaties; they are questions of war and of peace, of international law, and especially of principles of humanity. It is true that they involve definite violations of agreements, and especially of the Covenant of the League of Nations, the Briand-Kellogg Pact, and the Nine Power Treaty. But they also involve problems of world economy, world security, and world humanity.

It is true that the moral consciousness of the world must recognize the importance of removing injustices and well-founded grievances; but at the same time it must be aroused to the cardinal necessity of honoring sanctity of treaties, of respecting the rights and liberties of others, and of putting an end to acts of international aggression.

It seems to be unfortunately true that the epidemic of world lawlessness is spreading.

When an epidemic of physical disease starts to spread, the community approves and joins in a quarantine of the patients in order to protect the health of the community against the spread of the disease.

It is my determination to pursue a policy of peace and to adopt every practicable measure to avoid involvement in war. It ought to be inconceivable that in this modern era, and in the face of experience, any nation could be so foolish and ruthless as to run the risk of plunging the whole world into war by invading and violating in contravention of solemn treaties the territory of other nations that have done them no real harm and which are too weak to protect themselves adequately. Yet the peace of the world and the welfare and security of every nation is today being threatened by that very thing.

No nation which refuses to exercise forbearance and to respect the freedom and rights of others can long remain strong and retain the confidence and respect of other nations. No nation ever loses its dignity or good standing by conciliating its differences and by exercising great patience with and consideration for the rights of other nations.

War is a contagion, whether it be declared or undeclared. It can engulf states and peoples remote from the original scene of hostilities. We are determined to keep out of war, yet we cannot insure ourselves against the disastrous effects of war and the dangers of involvement. We are adopting such measures as will minimize our risk of involvement, but we cannot have complete protection in a world of disorder in which confidence and security have broken down.

If civilization is to survive the principles of the Prince of Peace must be restored. Shattered trust between nations must be revived.

Most important of all, the will for peace on the part of peace-loving nations must express itself to the end that nations that may be tempted to violate their agreements and the rights of others will desist from such a cause. There must be positive endeavors to preserve peace.

America hates war. America hopes for peace. Therefore, America actively engages in the search for peace.

PART IV

The United States in a World at War, II

(1940–1945)

THE outbreak of war in Europe caused a decline in American isolationism but did not result in its disappearance. The dangers of involvement in what some persons still described as the quarrels of other nations continued to be stressed (Selection 17). Nevertheless, the Administration succeeded in dismantling the neutrality legislation of the 1930's with considerable speed. When the fall of France made an Axis victory likely, the pace of American alignment with the European democracies quickened. By the end of 1940 President Roosevelt had in fact committed the United States to underwriting an Allied victory, though still only by means short of war (Selection 18).

In the meantime, the United States also sought to maintain its traditional policy of preventing the dominance of the Far East by a single strong power. This led to export restrictions and other moves designed to hamper Japan and to fruitless negotiations aimed at averting war in the Pacific without sacrificing American interests in the area (Selection 19).

When the Japanese attack on Pearl Harbor brought this country into the war, the stage was finally set for a fundamental reconsideration of American foreign policy. If American aloofness could not prevent war and if a general war seemed always likely to involve the United States, then American participation in a system of collective security was obviously called for. In the course of the Second World War, the United States officially

95

conceded for the first time that its foreign-policy interests extended beyond the winning of the war to the establishment of an international order for preserving peace (Selection 20).

Essential to the maintenance of international order was the continuation of the Grand Alliance, i.e., the continued cooperation between the United States, Great Britain, and the Soviet Union. As the war in Europe drew to a close, President Roosevelt sought to lay the basis for such future cooperation in direct negotiations with Churchill and Stalin and in formal agreement among the three powers (Selection 21). The United States thus moved from isolationism to acceptance of the collective security principle and consciously inaugurated a new era in its foreign relations.

17 / SENATOR TAFT REAFFIRMS
AMERICAN ISOLATIONISM

Even after Europe was at war and Hitler had conquered Poland, the ostensible lessons of the First World War were offered as arguments for American avoidance of "foreign quarrels." In a speech delivered in February 1940, Senator Robert A. Taft (1889–1953) of Ohio also repeated the same warnings which Representative Kitchin had given twenty-three years before. Significantly, Taft was far less adverse to intervention in the Pacific area than he was to involvement with the European powers.

Outside of North and South America today, we see a world at war. Implements of destruction predominate in Europe and in Asia. Cities and helpless civilians are bombed. Ships of bellig-

SOURCE: *Vital Speeches of the Day*, VI (March 1940), 345–48. Reprinted with permission.

erents and neutrals alike are sent to the bottom, often without warning, by mines, submarines and bombs. It is inevitable that our people are intensely interested in these contests, and intensely interested in the question of the extent to which they may affect their daily lives and the future of their children. There is real danger that the entire civilization of Europe, built up through thousands of years, with its historical landmarks and all its tremendous humanitarian accomplishments, may be utterly obliterated.

At the special session of Congress in October, we considered only questions of foreign policy. According to the peculiar rules of the Senate, debate was prolonged for six weeks on the amendments to the Neutrality Act, although everything that could be said was probably said in the first two weeks. But the delay served one great purpose—it encouraged and developed an intense debate throughout the nation on the question of American policy abroad. Serious differences of opinion developed as to the proper course which might tend to keep the United States out of the European war. Hardly two Senators took exactly the same viewpoint on all the amendments. But before the session ended it became apparent that the American people, above everything, were determined to keep out of war, and differed only as to the best methods. . . .

War is so horrible today that the reasons against it, unless forced by direct national interest are obvious to all. The glamour and romance of an earlier day, always largely imaginary, have been completely destroyed by the modern methods developed in the World War and since. No man wants to spend months or years himself in the trenches. Every parent dreads the day his or her sons might sail away to war.

But it is said that we cannot stay out, and maybe people still seem to feel that because we chose to participate in the World War we must inevitably be drawn into this war. Certainly we can stay out if we are determined and remain determined to do so. We have stayed out of many European wars. If we admit that we cannot stay out, we will be perpetually involved in war, for Europe's quarrels are everlasting. There is a welter of races there so confused that boundaries cannot be drawn without leaving minorities which are a perpetual source of friction. National animosities are traditional and bitter. Only in this country have they been laid aside and have the different races learned to live together in peace. In George Washington's Farewell Address there is one statement which is as true today as it was then. He said:

"Europe has a set of primary interests which to us have none or a very remote relation. Hence she must be engaged in frequent controversies, the causes of which are essentially foreign to our concerns."

It is difficult for us to know what is really going on in Europe, or the reasons which underlie the decisions of European governments. I have little sympathy with those who assume to judge all European statesmen, to criticize so-called power politics in Europe, who say in fact: "A plague on both your houses." There is just as much right and wrong in European quarrels as in any other quarrels.

When I see the freedom of independent nations like Czecho-Slovakia, Poland and Finland destroyed, my deepest sympathies are aroused in their behalf. It is contrary to human nature to have no sympathies between contesting European nations, but because we sympathize with one side is no reason why we should run onto the field and try to play in the game.

Of course we can stay out if we wish to do so. Holland and Switzerland stayed out of the World War, although they were in the very midst of it. We have an isolated position, and it is still isolated in spite of all the improvements on sea and in the air. In fact, developments in this war seem to show that effective aerial attack cannot be made over any considerable distance. I find that many people who say that we cannot stay out, at the bottom of their hearts do not wish to stay out. Certainly this argument presents no reason for not trying to stay out.

It has been widely argued that we should enter the war to defend democracies against dictatorships. The President's own expressions even this year have indicated a leaning to this belief. No one can sympathize more than I do with the success of democratic governments against dictatorships. No one desires more strongly than I the end of communism and Nazism, but I question whether war is the effective method of destroying them. Our experience in the World War did not indicate that we could interfere in European quarrels and work out any permanent or satisfactory solution. The World War did not even save democracy, but resulted in the creation of more dictatorships than the world has seen for many years. Nothing is so destructive of forms of government, particularly forms of democratic government, as war.

Our going to war would be more likely to destroy American democracy than to destroy German dictatorship. There are pending in Congress measures designed to have the government take over all business and property, fix prices and wages, and regulate every detail of private employment and commercial life. The President already has statutory power to take over the railroads and manufacturing plants in case of war, and the radios and public utilities in case of threatened war. I have little doubt that he would exercise most of these powers. . . .

I believe we will do the cause of democracy much more good if we maintain our neutrality, and show that a great nation can get through a crisis of this kind without abandoning democratic principles. There is only one way to spread democracy throughout the world—that is by showing the people that under democratic government they are more likely to have peace and happiness than under any other form. Democracy spread through the world in the nineteenth century from our example, and it can do so again.

The horrors of a modern war are so great, its futility is so evident, its effect on prosperity and happiness, and democratic government itself, so destructive, that any alternative seems to be preferable except the subjection of this country to physical attack or the loss of its freedom. . . .

The Far Eastern situation presents an even more difficult problem. . . .

While it is not nearly so dangerous to become involved in a war in the Pacific as in the European war, I believe our people desire to avoid any such probability. Frankly, I have not been able to make up my own mind how far the United States can go in assisting China against an unwarranted attack without becoming involved in war itself. A war in the Pacific is even more to be avoided while war exists in Europe, for the two are not likely to remain completely separate and apart.

18 / PRESIDENT FRANKLIN D. ROOSEVELT ALIGNS AMERICA WITH BRITAIN

After the fall of France and the formation of the Rome-Berlin-Tokyo Axis, President Roosevelt reached the conclusion that the combined power of these nations represented a very real threat to the security of the United States. Having already asked for and secured modification of the Neutrality Act and the first peacetime selective service act in American history, he used a fireside chat on December 29, 1940, to announce that he regarded the cause of Great Britain that of the United States. While opposing American armed intervention, he insisted that, in order to protect its own interests, the United States "must become the great arsenal of democracy."

Never before since Jamestown and Plymouth Rock has our American civilization been in such danger as now.

For, on September 27, 1940, by an agreement signed in Berlin, three powerful nations, two in Europe and one in Asia, joined themselves together in the threat that if the United States interfered with or blocked the expansion program of these three nations—a program aimed at world control—they would unite in ultimate action against the United States.

The Nazi masters of Germany have made it clear that they

SOURCE: Department of State, *Peace and War: United States Foreign Policy, 1931–1941* (Washington: Government Printing Office, 1941), pp. 599–608.

intend not only to dominate all life and thought in their own country, but also to enslave the whole of Europe, and then to use the resources of Europe to dominate the rest of the world. . . .

In view of the nature of this undeniable threat, it can be asserted, properly and categorically, that the United States has no right or reason to encourage talk of peace until the day shall come when there is a clear intention on the part of the aggressor nations to abandon all thought of dominating or conquering the world.

At this moment, the forces of the states that are leagued against all peoples who live in freedom are being held away from our shores. The Germans and Italians are being blocked on the other side of the Atlantic by the British, and by the Greeks, and by thousands of soldiers and sailors who were able to escape from subjugated countries. The Japanese are being engaged in Asia by the Chinese in another great defense.

In the Pacific is our fleet.

Some of our people like to believe that wars in Europe and in Asia are of no concern to us. But it is a matter of most vital concern to us that European and Asiatic war-makers should not gain control of the oceans which lead to this hemisphere.

One hundred and seventeen years ago the Monroe Doctrine was conceived by our Government as a measure of defense in the face of a threat against this hemisphere by an alliance in continental Europe. Thereafter, we stood on guard in the Atlantic, with the British as neighbors. There was no treaty. There was no "unwritten agreement."

Yet, there was the feeling, proven correct by history, that we as neighbors could settle any disputes in peaceful fashion. The fact is that during the whole of this time the Western Hemisphere has remained free from aggression from Europe or from Asia.

Does anyone seriously believe that we need to fear attack while a free Britain remains our most powerful naval neighbor in the Atlantic? Does any one seriously believe, on the other hand, that we could rest easy if the Axis powers were our neighbor there?

If Great Britain goes down, the Axis powers will control the continents of Europe, Asia, Africa, Australasia, and the high seas —and they will be in a position to bring enormous military and naval resources against this hemisphere. It is no exaggeration to say that all of us in the Americas would be living at the point of a gun—a gun loaded with explosive bullets, economic as well as military.

We should enter upon a new and terrible era in which the whole world, our hemisphere included, would be run by threats of brute force. To survive in such a world, we would have to convert ourselves permanently into a militaristic power on the basis of war economy.

Some of us like to believe that even if Great Britain falls, we are still safe, because of the broad expanse of the Atlantic and of the Pacific.

But the width of these oceans is not what it was in the days of clipper ships. At one point between Africa and Brazil the distance is less than from Washington to Denver—five hours for the latest type of bomber. And at the north of the Pacific Ocean, America and Asia almost touch each other.

Even today we have planes which could fly from the British Isles to New England and back without refueling. And the range of the modern bomber is ever being increased. . . .

Frankly and definitely there is danger ahead—danger against which we must prepare. But we well know that we cannot escape danger, or the fear of it, by crawling into bed and pulling the covers over our heads.

Some nations of Europe were bound by solemn non-intervention pacts with Germany. Other nations were assured by Germany that they need never fear invasion. Non-intervention pact or not, the fact remains that they were attacked, overrun, and thrown into the modern form of slavery at an hour's notice or even without any notice at all. . . .

The experience of the past two years has proven beyond doubt that no nation can appease the Nazis. No man can tame a tiger into a kitten by stroking it. There can be no appeasement with ruthlessness. There can be no reasoning with an incendiary bomb. We know now that a nation can have peace with the Nazis only at the price of total surrender.

Even the people of Italy have been forced to become accomplices of the Nazis; but at this moment they do not know how soon they will be embraced to death by their allies.

The American appeasers ignore the warning to be found in the fate of Austria, Czechoslovakia, Poland, Norway, Belgium, the Netherlands, Denmark, and France. They tell you that the Axis powers are going to win anyway; that all this bloodshed in the world could be saved; and that the United States might just as well throw its influence into the scale of a dictated peace, and get the best out of it that we can.

They call it a "negotiated peace." Nonsense! Is it a negotiated peace if a gang of outlaws surrounds your community and on threat of extermination makes you pay tribute to save your own skins?

Such a dictated peace would be no peace at all. It would be only another armistice, leading to the most gigantic armament race and the most devastating trade wars in history. And in these contests the Americas would offer the only real resistance to the Axis powers.

With all their vaunted efficiency and parade of pious purpose in this war, there are still in their background the concentration camp and the servants of God in chains.

The history of recent years proves that shootings and chains and concentration camps are not simply the transient tools but the very altars of modern dictatorships. They may talk of a "new order" in the world, but what they have in mind is but a revival of the oldest and the worst tyranny. In that there is no liberty, no religion, no hope.

The proposed "new order" is the very opposite of a United States of Europe or a United States of Asia. It is not a government based upon the consent of the governed. It is not a union of ordinary, self-respecting men and women to protect themselves and their freedom and their dignity from oppression. It is an unholy alliance of power and pelf to dominate and enslave the human race.

The British people are conducting an active war against this unholy alliance. Our own future security is greatly dependent on the outcome of that fight. Our ability to "keep out of war" is going to be affected by that outcome.

Thinking in terms of today and tomorrow, I make the direct statement to the American people that there is far less chance of the United States getting into war if we do all we can now to support the nations defending themselves against attack by the Axis than if we acquiesce in their defeat, submit tamely to an Axis victory, and wait our turn to be the object of attack in another war later on.

If we are to be completely honest with ourselves, we must admit there is risk in *any* course we may take. But I deeply believe that the great majority of our people agree that the course that I advocate involves the least risk now and the greatest hope for world peace in the future.

The people of Europe who are defending themselves do not ask us to do their fighting. They ask us for the implements of war, the planes, the tanks, the guns, the freighters, which will enable them to fight for their liberty and our security. Emphatically we must get these weapons to them in sufficient volume and quickly enough, so that we and our children will be saved the agony and suffering of war which others have had to endure.

Let not defeatists tell us that it is too late. It will never be earlier. Tomorrow will be later than today.

Certain facts are self-evident.

In a military sense Great Britain and the British Empire are today the spearhead of resistance to world conquest. They are putting up a fight which will live forever in the story of human gallantry.

There is no demand for sending an American Expeditionary Force outside our own borders. There is no intention by any member of your Government to send such a force. You can, therefore, nail any talk about sending armies to Europe as deliberate untruth.

Our national policy is not directed toward war. Its sole purpose is to keep war away from our country and our people.

Democracy's fight against world conquest is being greatly

aided, and must be more greatly aided, by the rearmament of the United States and by sending every ounce and every ton of munitions and supplies that we can possibly spare to help the defenders who are in the front lines. It is no more unneutral for us to do that than it is for Sweden, Russia, and other nations near Germany to send steel and ore and oil and other war materials into Germany every day.

We are planning our own defense with the utmost urgency; and in its vast scale we must integrate the war needs of Britain and the other free nations resisting aggression. . . .

As planes and ships and guns and shells are produced, your Government, with its defense experts, can then determine how best to use them to defend this hemisphere. The decision as to how much shall be sent abroad and how much shall remain at home must be made on the basis of our over-all military necessities.

We must be the great arsenal of democracy. For us this is an emergency as serious as war itself. We must apply ourselves to our task with the same resolution, the same sense of urgency, the same spirit of patriotism and sacrifice, as we would show were we at war.

19 / THE UNITED STATES AND JAPAN CLASH IN THE PACIFIC

The continuing Japanese advance into China and the occupation of Indochina in July 1941 brought American protests and commercial discrimination. The United States felt compelled both to protect its own interests in the Far East and to support the interests of Great Britain, France, and the Netherlands, to whose cause in Europe this country was already largely committed. Joseph P. Ballantine's memorandum on a meeting between Secretary of State Hull and the Japanese representatives Nomura and Kurusu shows the unsatisfactory stage which negotiations had reached. The meeting took place on December 1, 1941, the day on which a secret Imperial Conference approved a decision to go to war without formal declaration, thus paving the way for the Pearl Harbor attack.

The Secretary [Cordell Hull] said that he had been talking peace for nine months with the Japanese Ambassador [Admiral Kichisaburo Nomura], both of them acting in entire good faith. He said that during all the time that [Japanese Foreign Minister Yosuke] Matsuoka was holding forth on the Tripartite Alliance and engaging in general bluster, the Secretary had ignored all of that. Then while the talks were in progress last July the Japanese moved suddenly into Indochina without any advance notice to this Government, and possibly the Ambassador was not informed of the Japanese Government's intention in advance. Then, too, the Secretary said, the Japanese press had been con-

SOURCE: Department of State, *Peace and War: United States Foreign Policy, 1931–1941* (Washington: Government Printing Office, 1941), pp. 817–22.

ducting a blustering campaign against the United States. The Secretary said that this Government had no idea of trying to bluff Japan and he saw no occasion for Japan's trying to bluff us, and he emphasized that there is a limit beyond which we cannot go further and that one of these days we may reach a point when we cannot keep on as we are.

Mr. [Saburo] Kurusu [special envoy to the United States] said that the Japanese Government had been very much surprised at the reaction in this country to the Prime Minister's statements and he would see to it that the Secretary was given a correct translation of the Prime Minister's statements. . . . He then said that the Japanese Government believed that the proposal which they submitted to us on November 20 was equitable and that full consideration had been given therein to the points of view taken by both sides in the conversations; that the Japanese Government finds it difficult to understand the position taken by the Government of the United States; and that the proposal which we had communicated to them seemed to fail to take cognizance of the actual conditions in the Far East. He said that his Government directed him to inquire what was the ultimate aim of the United States in the conversations and to request this Government to make "deep reflection of this matter." Mr. Kurusu said that the Japanese offer to withdraw its troops from southern Indochina still stands; that Japan has shown its extreme desire to promote a peaceful settlement.

The Secretary replied that we had to take into account the bellicose utterances emanating from Tokyo and that never would there be possible any peaceful arrangements if such arrangements have to be based upon principles of force. He pointed out that the methods the Japanese are using in China are similar to those which are being adopted by Hitler to subjugate Europe. The Secretary said that he had called attention to that during the progress of our conversations and that we cannot lose sight of the movement by Hitler to seize one-half of the world. He said that we believe that the Japanese militarists are moving in a similar direction to seize the other half of the earth, and that this Government cannot yield to anything of that kind. He explained that this is why we desire to work things out in a way that would promote peace, stability and prosperity and that this is why he has thus far made no complaint, notwithstanding the fact that the Japanese press has heaped filthy abuse on this country.

The Ambassador expressed the view that as a matter of fact there is not much difference between Japan's idea of a co-prosperity sphere and Pan-Americanism, except that Japanese methods may be more primitive. He denied that it was Japan's purpose to use force. The Secretary asked whether, when the Japanese Government was moving on the territory of other countries, inch by inch by force, the Ambassador thought that this was a part of our policy. The Ambassador replied that Japan was motivated by self-defense in the same way as Britain had been motivated by her acts, for example, in Syria; that Japan needed rice and other materials at a time when she was being shut off by the United States and other countries and she had no alternative but to endeavor to obtain access to these materials.

The Secretary observed that the Japanese are saying that the United States has no right to interfere with what Japan is doing in eastern Asia; that when the Japanese keep their troops in Indochina this constitutes a menace to the South Sea area, ir-respective of where in Indochina the troops are stationed; that the stationing of these troops in Indochina is making it necessary for the United States and its friends to keep large numbers of armed forces immobilized in east Asia, and in this way Japan's acts were having the effect of aiding Hitler. The Secretary reminded the Ambassador that he had made it clear to the Ambassador that we could not sit still while such developments were taking place.

The Ambassador commented that today war is being con-ducted through the agency of economic weapons, that Japan was being squeezed, and that Japan must expand to obtain raw mate-rials. The Secretary pointed out that we were selling Japan oil until Japan suddenly moved into Indochina; that he could not defend such a situation indefinitely; and that the United States would give Japan all she wanted in the way of materials if Japan's military leaders would only show that Japan intended to pursue a peaceful course. The Secretary emphasized that we do not propose to go into partnership with Japan's military leaders; that he has not heard one whisper of peace from the Japanese military, only bluster and blood-curdling threats. The Secretary added that he had been subjected to very severe criticism for his policy of patience but that he would not mind if only the Japanese Government could back him up. . . .

. . . The Secretary went on to say that under existing circumstances, when Japan was tied in with the Tripartite Pact, Japan might just as well ask us to cease aiding Britain as to cease aiding China. He emphasized again that we can't overlook Japan's digging herself into Indochina, the effect of which is to create an increasing menace to America and her friends; that we can't continue to take chances on the situation; and that we will not allow ourselves to be kicked out of the Pacific. . . .

The Secretary pointed out that every time we get started in the direction of progress the Japanese military does something to overturn us. The Secretary expressed grave doubts whether we could now get ahead in view of all the threats that had been made. He pointed out that the acts of the Japanese militarists had effectively tied the hands of the Ambassadors and he did not know whether the Ambassadors could succeed in having anything accomplished toward untying their hands. Mr. Kurusu brought up again his contention made on previous occasions that China had taken advantage of the Washington Conference treaties to flaunt Japan, and commented that if we don't look out China will sell both the United States and Japan down the river. The Secretary observed that he has been plowing through various contradictions in Japanese acts and utterances. He pointed out that the Japanese had been telling us that if something quick is not done something awful was about to happen; that they kept urging upon the Secretary the danger of delay, and kept pressing the Secretary to do something. He said that in view of all the confusion, threats and pressure, he had been brought to the stage where he felt that something must be done to clear the foggy atmosphere; that his conclusion was that he must bring us back to fundamentals; and that these fundamentals were embodied in the proposal which we had offered the Japanese on November 26. He said that we have stood from the first on the points involved in this proposal. He pointed out that everything that Japan was doing and saying was in precisely the opposite direction from the course we have been talking about in our conversations, and that these should be reversed by his government before we can further seriously talk peace.

Mr. Kurusu endeavored to make some lame apology for the direct military mind of the Japanese Army and commented that General Tojo was in position to control the situation. The Secretary asked what possibility there was of peace-minded people coming out in Japan and expressing themselves. He expressed doubt whether anybody in Japan would be free to speak unless he preached conquest. The Ambassador commented that the Japanese people are not talking about conquest. The Secretary pointed out that we all understand what are the implications of such terms as "controlling influence," "new order in east Asia," and "co-prosperity sphere." The Secretary observed that Hitler was using similar terms as synonyms for purposes of conquest. The Secretary went on to say that there was no reason for conflict between the United States and Japan, that there was no real clash of interest. He added that Japan does not have to use a sword to gain for herself a seat at the head of the table. He pointed out that equality of opportunity is in our opinion the key to the future peace and prosperity of all nations.

Mr. Kurusu disclaimed on the part of Japan any similarity between Japan's purposes and Hitler's purposes. The Ambassador pointed out that wars never settle anything and that war in the Pacific would be a tragedy, but he added that the Japanese people believe that the United States wants to keep Japan fighting with China and to keep Japan strangled. He said that the Japanese people feel that they are faced with the alternative of surrendering to the United States or of fighting. The Ambassador said that he was still trying to save the situation. The Secretary said that he has practically exhausted himself here, that the American people are going to assume that there is real danger to this country in the situation, and that there is nothing he can do to prevent it.

20 / SECRETARY OF STATE HULL
AWAKENS TO INTERNATIONALISM

*American commitment to the principle of collective
security was manifested in the Declaration of the United
Nations on January 1, 1942. That this represented a
permanent departure from isolationism and a firm
commitment not only to the winning of the war but
also to the establishment, in concert with other
nations, of a stable world order based on formal
international cooperation was made clear in a radio
speech delivered by Secretary of State Cordell Hull
(1871–1955) on April 9, 1944, the fourth anniversary
of Hitler's invasion of Denmark and Norway.*

In talking about foreign policy it is well to remember, as Justice
Holmes said, that a page of history is worth a volume of logic.
There are three outstanding lessons in our recent history to
which I particularly wish to draw your attention. In the first
place, since the outbreak of the present war in Europe, we and
those nations who are now our allies have moved from relative
weakness to strength. In the second place, during that same
period we in this country have moved from a deep-seated tendency toward separate action to the knowledge and conviction
that only through unity of action can there be achieved in this
world the results which are essential for the continuance of free
peoples. And, thirdly, we have moved from a careless tolerance
of evil institutions to the conviction that free governments and
Nazi and Fascist governments cannot exist together in this world
because the very nature of the latter requires them to be aggres-

SOURCE: *Department of State Bulletin*, X (April 15, 1944), 335–42.

sors and the very nature of free governments too often lays them open to treacherous and well-laid plans of attack.

An understanding of these points will help to clarify the policy which this Government has been and is following.

In 1940, with the fall of France, the peoples of the free world awoke with horror to find themselves on the very brink of defeat. Only Britain in the west and China in the east stood between them and disaster, and the space on which they stood was narrow and precarious. At that moment the free nations were militarily weak, and their enemies and potential enemies were strong and well prepared. Even before that this country had begun its preparations for self-defense. Soon thereafter we started upon the long hard road of mobilizing our great natural resources, our vast productive potentialities, and our reserves of manpower to defend ourselves and to strengthen those who were resisting the aggressors. . . .

This decision which we have made and carried out was not a decision to make a mere sporadic effort. An episode is not a policy. The American people are determined to press forward with our Allies to the defeat of our enemies and the destruction of the Nazi and Fascist systems which plunged us into the war. And they are also determined to go on, after the victory, with our Allies and all other nations which desire peace and freedom to establish and maintain in full strength the institutions without which peace and freedom cannot be an enduring reality. We cannot move in and out of international cooperation and in and out of participation in the responsibilities of a member of the family of nations. The political, material, and spiritual strength of the free and democratic nations not only is greatly dependent upon the strength which our full participation brings to the common effort but, as we now know, is a vital factor in our own strength. As it is with the keystone of an arch, neither the keystone nor the arch can stand alone. . . .

As I look at the map of Europe, certain things seem clear to me. As the Nazis go down to defeat they will inevitably leave behind them in Germany and the satellite states of southeastern Europe a legacy of confusion. It is essential that we and our Allies establish the controls necessary to bring order out of this chaos as rapidly as possible and do everything possible to prevent its spread to the German-occupied countries of eastern and western Europe while they are in the throes of reestablishing government and repairing the most brutal ravages of the war. If confusion should spread throughout Europe it is difficult to over-emphasize the seriousness of the disaster that may follow. Therefore, for us, for the world, and for the countries concerned, a stable Europe should be an immediate objective of allied policy.

Stability and order do not and cannot mean reaction. Order there must be to avoid chaos. But it must be achieved in a manner which will give full scope to men and women who look forward, men and women who will end Fascism and all its works and create the institutions of a free and democratic way of life.

We look with hope and with deep faith to a period of great democratic accomplishment in Europe. Liberation from the German yoke will give the peoples of Europe a new and magnificent opportunity to fulfill their democratic aspirations, both in building democratic political institutions of their own choice and in achieving the social and economic democracy on which political democracy must rest. It is important to our national interest to encourage the establishment in Europe of strong and progressive popular governments, dedicated like our own to improving the social welfare of the people as a whole—governments which will join the common effort of nations in creating the conditions of lasting peace and in promoting the expansion of production, employment, and the exchange and consumption of goods, which are the material foundations of the liberty and welfare of all peoples. . . .

. . . After two years of intensive study, the basis upon which our policy must be founded is soundly established; the direction is clear; and the general methods of accomplishment are emerging.

This basis of policy and these methods rest upon the second of the lessons which I said at the outset of my remarks was found in the pages of our recent history. It is that action upon these matters cannot be separate but must be agreed and united action. This is fundamental. It must underlie the entire range of our policy. The free nations have been brought to the very brink of destruction by allowing themselves to be separated and divided. If any lesson has ever been hammered home with blood and suffering, that one has been. And the lesson is not yet ended.

However difficult the road may be, there is no hope of turning victory into enduring peace unless the real interests of this country, the British Commonwealth, the Soviet Union, and China are harmonized and unless they agree and act together. This is the solid framework upon which all future policy and international organization must be built. It offers the fullest opportunity for the development of institutions in which all free nations may participate democratically, through which a reign of law and morality may arise, and through which the material interests of all may be advanced. But without an enduring understanding between these four nations upon their fundamental purposes, interests, and obligations to one another, all organizations to preserve peace are creations on paper and the path is wide open again for the rise of a new aggressor.

This essential understanding and unity of action among the four nations is not in substitution or derogation of unity among the United Nations. But it is basic to all organized international action because upon its reality depends the possibility of enduring peace and free institutions rather than new coalitions and a new pre-war period. Nor do I suggest that any conclusion of these four nations can or should be without the participation of the other United Nations. I am stating what I believe the common sense of my fellow countrymen and all men will recognize —that for these powers to become divided in their aims and fail to recognize and harmonize their basic interests can produce only disaster and that no machinery, as such, can produce this essential harmony and unity. . . .

Although the road to unity of purpose and action is long and difficult we have taken long strides upon our way. The Atlantic Charter was proclaimed by the President and the Prime Minister of Great Britain in August 1941. Then, by the Declaration of the United Nations of January 1, 1942, these nations adopted the principles of the Atlantic Charter, agreed to devote all their resources to the winning of the war, and pledged themselves not to conclude a separate armistice or peace with their common enemies.

After that came the declaration signed at Moscow on October 30, 1943. Here the four nations who are carrying and must carry the chief burden of defeating their enemies renewed their determination by joint action to achieve this end. But they went further than this and pledged cooperation with one another to establish at the earliest practicable date, with other peace-loving states, an effective international organization to maintain peace and security, which in principle met with overwhelming nonpartisan approval by the Congress in the Connally and Fulbright resolutions.

Further steps along the road of united allied action were taken at the conference at Cairo, where the President and Mr. Churchill met with Generalissimo Chiang Kai-shek, and at the conference at Tehran, where they met with Marshal Stalin. At Tehran the three Allies fighting in Europe reached complete agreement on military plans for winning the war and made plain their determination to achieve harmonious action in the period of peace. That concert among the Allies rests on broad foundations of common interests and common aspirations, and it will endure. . . .

May I close with a word as to the responsibility which rests upon us. The United Nations will determine by action or lack of action whether this world will be visited by another war within the next 20 or 25 years, or whether policies of organized peace shall guide the course of the world. We are moving closer and closer to the hour of decision. Only the fullest measure of wisdom, unity, and alertness can enable us to meet that unprecedented responsibility. . . .

. . . Once before in our lifetime we fell into disunity and became ineffective in world affairs by reason of it. Should this happen again it will be a tragedy to you and to your children and to the world for generations.

21 / THE UNITED STATES STRIVES TO MAINTAIN THE GRAND ALLIANCE

For the principle of collective security to be effective in the postwar world, it was essential that cooperation between the two remaining major powers, the United States and the Soviet Union, be maintained. The Yalta Agreement of February 11, 1945, was the major American effort to maintain such cooperation in the face of mounting evidence that future dealings with the Soviet Union would be less than successful. The United States was able to secure both a Russian promise to aid in the defeat of Japan and a commitment to participate in the work of the United Nations Organization.

The following statement is made by the Prime Minister of Great Britain, the President of the United States of America, and the Chairman of the Council of Peoples' Commissars of the Union of Soviet Socialist Republics on the results of the Crimean Conference:

I. THE DEFEAT OF GERMANY

We have considered and determined the military plans of the three allied powers for the final defeat of the common enemy. The military staffs of the three allied nations have met in daily meetings throughout the Conference. These meetings have been

SOURCE: *Papers Relating to the Foreign Relations of the United States: The Conferences at Malta and Yalta* (Washington: Government Printing Office, 1955), pp. 968–75, 984.

most satisfactory from every point of view and have resulted in closer coordination of the military effort of the three Allies than ever before. The fullest information has been inter-changed. The timing, scope and coordination of new and even more powerful blows to be launched by our armies and air forces into the heart of Germany from the East, West, North and South have been fully agreed and planned in detail. . . .

Nazi Germany is doomed. The German people will only make the cost of their defeat heavier to themselves by attempting to continue a hopeless resistance.

II. The Occupation and Control of Germany

We have agreed on common policies and plans for enforcing the unconditional surrender terms which we shall impose together on Nazi Germany after German armed resistance has been finally crushed. . . .

It is our inflexible purpose to destroy German militarism and Nazism and to ensure that Germany will never again be able to disturb the peace of the world. We are determined to disarm and disband all German armed forces; break up for all time the German General Staff that has repeatedly contrived the resurgence of German militarism; remove or destroy all German military equipment; eliminate or control all German industry that could be used for military production; bring all war criminals to just and swift punishment and exact reparation in kind for the destruction wrought by the Germans; wipe out the Nazi party, Nazi laws, organizations and institutions, remove all Nazi and militarist influences from public office and from the cultural and economic life of the German people; and take in harmony such other measures in Germany as may be necessary to the future peace and safety of the world. It is not our purpose to destroy the people of Germany, but only when Nazism and Militarism have been extirpated will there be hope for a decent life for Germans, and a place for them in the comity of nations.

III. REPARATION BY GERMANY

We have considered the question of the damage caused by Germany to the Allied Nations in this war and recognized it as just that Germany be obliged to make compensation for this damage in kind to the greatest extent possible. . . .

IV. UNITED NATIONS CONFERENCE

We are resolved upon the earliest possible establishment with our allies of a general international organization to maintain peace and security. We believe that this is essential, both to prevent aggression and to remove the political, economic and social causes of war through the close and continuing collaboration of all peace-loving peoples.

The foundations were laid at Dumbarton Oaks. On the important question of voting procedure, however, agreement was not there reached. The present conference has been able to resolve this difficulty.

We have agreed that a Conference of United Nations should be called to meet at San Francisco in the United States on April 25th, 1945, to prepare the charter of such an organization, along the lines proposed in the informal conversations at Dumbarton Oaks. . . .

V. DECLARATION ON LIBERATED EUROPE

We have drawn up and subscribed to a Declaration on liberated Europe. This Declaration provides for concerting the policies of the three Powers and for joint action by them in meeting the political and economic problems of liberated Europe in accordance with democratic principles. The text of the Declaration is as follows:

The Premier of the Union of Soviet Socialist Republics, the Prime Minister of the United Kingdom, and the President of the United States of America have consulted with each other in the common interests of the peoples of their countries and those of liberated Europe. They jointly declare their mutual agreement to concert during the temporary period of instability in liberated Europe the policies of their three governments in assisting the peoples liberated from the domination of Nazi Germany and the peoples of the former Axis satellite states of Europe to solve by democratic means their pressing political and economic problems.

The establishment of order in Europe and the rebuilding of national economic life must be achieved by processes which will enable the liberated peoples to destroy the last vestiges of Nazism and Fascism and to creat[e] democratic institutions of their own choice. This is a principle of the Atlantic Charter— the right of all peoples to choose the form of government under which they will live—the restoration of sovereign rights and self-government to those peoples who have been forcibly deprived of them by the aggressor nations.

To foster the conditions in which the liberated peoples may exercise these rights, the three governments will jointly assist the people in any European liberated state or former Axis satellite state in Europe where in their judgment conditions require (a) to establish conditions of internal peace; (b) to carry out emergency measures for the relief of distressed people; (c) to form interim governmental authorities broadly representative of all democratic elements in the population and pledged to the earliest possible establishment through free elections of governments responsive to the will of the people; and (d) to facilitate where necessary the holding of such elections.

The three governments will consult the other United Nations and provisional authorities or other governments in Europe when matters of direct interest to them are under consideration.

When, in the opinion of the three governments, conditions in any European liberated state or any former Axis satellite state in Europe make such action necessary, they will immediately consult together on the measures necessary to discharge the joint responsibilities set forth in this declaration.

By this declaration we reaffirm our faith in the principles of the Atlantic Charter, our pledge in the Declaration by the United Nations, and our determination to build in cooperation with other peace-loving nations a world order under law, dedicated to peace, security, freedom and the general well-being of all mankind. . . .

VI. POLAND

We came to the Crimea Conference resolved to settle our differences about Poland. We discussed fully all aspects of the question. We reaffirm our common desire to see established a strong, free, independent and democratic Poland. . . .

. . . . .

VIII. MEETINGS OF FOREIGN SECRETARIES

Throughout the Conference, besides the daily meetings of the Heads of Governments and the Foreign Secretaries, separate meetings of the three Foreign Secretaries and their advisers have also been held daily.

These meetings have proved of the utmost value and the Conference agreed that permanent machinery should be set up for regular consultation between the three Foreign Secretaries. They will, therefore, meet as often as may be necessary, probably about every three or four months. These meetings will be held in rotation in the three Capitals, the first meeting being held in London, after the United Nations Conference on world organization.

IX. UNITY FOR PEACE AS FOR WAR

Our meeting here in the Crimea has reaffirmed our common determination to maintain and strengthen in the peace to come that unity of purpose and of action which has made victory possible and certain for the United Nations in this war. We believe that this is a sacred obligation which our Governments owe to our peoples and to all the peoples of the world.

Only with continuing and growing co-operation and understanding among our three countries and among all the peace-loving nations can the highest aspiration of humanity be realized —a secure and lasting peace which will, in the words of the

Atlantic Charter, "afford assurance that all the men in all the lands may live out their lives in freedom from fear and want."

Victory in this war and establishment of the proposed international organization will provide the greatest opportunity in all history to create in the years to come the essential conditions of such a peace.

.   .   .   .   .

AGREEMENT

The leaders of the three Great Powers—the Soviet Union, the United States of America and Great Britain—have agreed that in two or three months after Germany has surrendered and the war in Europe has terminated the Soviet Union shall enter into the war against Japan on the side of the Allies on condition that:

1. The *status quo* in Outer-Mongolia (The Mongolian People's Republic) shall be preserved;

2. The former rights of Russia violated by the treacherous attack of Japan in 1904 shall be restored . . . ;

3. The Kuril islands shall be handed over to the Soviet Union.

It is understood, that the agreement concerning Outer-Mongolia and the ports and railroads referred to above will require concurrence of Generalissimo Chiang Kai-Shek. The President will take measures in order to obtain this concurrence on advice from Marshal Stalin.

The Heads of the three Great Powers have agreed that these claims of the Soviet Union shall be unquestionably fulfilled after Japan has been defeated.

For its part the Soviet Union expresses its readiness to conclude with the National Government of China a pact of friendship and alliance between the USSR and China in order to render assistance to China with its armed forces for the purpose of liberating China from the Japanese yoke.

PART V

The United States and the Cold War

(1947–1954)

W<small>HEN</small> the Soviet Union failed to live up to the Yalta and Potsdam Agreements and the other European powers proved too weak to assume international responsibilities, the concept of collective security turned out to be unworkable. The United States thereupon moved consciously to assume the burdens of world leadership. The Truman Doctrine (Selection 22) committed the United States firmly to the defense of the West against both aggression and subversion, and the theories of George Kennan (Selection 23) became the basis for a policy designed primarily to prevent the further expansion of the territory and the sphere of influence of the Soviet Union.

Challenges to this policy, particularly the Berlin blockade, and American response to these challenges tended to shift the focus of United States foreign policy from the traditional areas, the Caribbean and the Far East, almost entirely to Europe and the adjacent Near East (Selection 24). When this produced a new challenge in the Pacific by the invasion of South Korea, critics of American foreign policy were quick to attack the scope of the commitments the United States had assumed and to urge a return to something like the traditional policies of the pre-World War II period (Selection 25).

Though such criticism produced no concrete results, the containment policy eventually proved unsatisfactory even to its advocates, since it seemed to offer no solutions to world problems beyond the permanent continuation of the Cold War. As a result, the United States at least tentatively considered a policy designed to shrink the Communist orbit by "liberating" various peoples dominated by the Soviet Union or, alternatively, to rely in a continuing Cold War on something less complicated and difficult than the maintenance of American military outposts throughout the world (Selection 26).

In the final analysis, however, America's foreign-policy posture was affected less by projections made in Washington than by the shift in leadership in the Soviet Union and the resultant changes which took place within the Soviet orbit.

22 / PRESIDENT TRUMAN PROCLAIMS A DOCTRINE

The failure of the Soviet Union to abide by the Yalta Agreement and the general breakdown of international cooperation after World War II led President Harry S Truman (1884–) to announce the second major shift in American foreign policy in a decade. Reacting directly to Soviet involvement in the Greek civil war and to the pressure applied on Turkey, he appeared before Congress on March 12, 1947, to proclaim what came to be called the Truman Doctrine: the commitment of the United States to support, with arms and money, "free peoples who are resisting attempted subjugation by armed minorities or by outside pressure."

The gravity of the situation which confronts the world today necessitates my appearance before a joint session of the Congress.

SOURCE: *Department of State Bulletin,* XVI (March 23, 1947), 534–37.

The foreign policy and the national security of this country are involved.

One aspect of the present situation, which I wish to present to you at this time for your consideration and decision, concerns Greece and Turkey.

The United States has received from the Greek Government an urgent appeal for financial and economic assistance. Preliminary reports from the American Economic Mission now in Greece and reports from the American Ambassador in Greece corroborate the statement of the Greek Government that assistance is imperative if Greece is to survive as a free nation.

I do not believe that the American people and the Congress wish to turn a deaf ear to the appeal of the Greek Government. . . .

The very existence of the Greek state is today threatened by the terrorist activities of several thousand armed men, led by Communists, who defy the Government's authority at a number of points, particularly along the northern boundaries. A commission appointed by the United Nations Security Council is at present investigating disturbed conditions in northern Greece and alleged border violations along the frontier between Greece on the one hand and Albania, Bulgaria, and Yugoslavia on the other.

Meanwhile, the Greek Government is unable to cope with the situation. The Greek Army is small and poorly equipped. It needs supplies and equipment if it is to restore authority to the Government throughout Greek territory.

Greece must have assistance if it is to become a self-supporting and self-respecting democracy. The United States must supply that assistance. We have already extended to Greece certain types of relief and economic aid, but these are inadequate. There is no other country to which democratic Greece can turn.

No other nation is willing and able to provide the necessary support for a democratic Greek Government.

The British Government, which has been helping Greece, can give no further financial or economic aid after March 31. Great Britain finds itself under the necessity of reducing or liquidating its commitments in several parts of the world, including Greece.

We have considered how the United Nations might assist in this crisis. But the situation is an urgent one requiring immediate action, and the United Nations and its related organizations are not in a position to extend help of the kind that is required. . . .

Greece's neighbor, Turkey, also deserves our attention.

The future of Turkey as an independent and economically sound state is clearly no less important to the freedom-loving peoples of the world than the future of Greece. The circumstances in which Turkey finds itself today are considerably different from those of Greece. Turkey has been spared the disasters that have beset Greece. And during the war the United States and Great Britain furnished Turkey with material aid.

Nevertheless, Turkey now needs our support.

Since the war Turkey has sought additional financial assistance from Great Britain and the United States for the purpose of effecting that modernization necessary for the maintenance of its national integrity.

That integrity is essential to the preservation of order in the Middle East.

The British Government has informed us that, owing to its own difficulties, it can no longer extend financial or economic aid to Turkey.

As in the case of Greece, if Turkey is to have the assistance it needs, the United States must supply it. We are the only country able to provide that help.

I am fully aware of the broad implications involved if the United States extends assistance to Greece and Turkey, and I shall discuss these implications with you at this time.

One of the primary objectives of the foreign policy of the United States is the creation of conditions in which we and other nations will be able to work out a way of life free from coercion. This was a fundamental issue in the war with Germany and Japan. Our victory was won over countries which sought to impose their will, and their way of life, upon other nations.

To insure the peaceful development of nations, free from coercion, the United States has taken a leading part in establishing the United Nations. The United Nations is designed to make possible lasting freedom and independence for all its members. We shall not realize our objectives, however, unless we are willing to help free peoples to maintain their free institutions and their national integrity against aggressive movements that seek to impose upon them totalitarian regimes. This is no more than a frank recognition that totalitarian regimes imposed upon free peoples, by direct or indirect aggression, undermine the foundations of international peace and hence the security of the United States.

The peoples of a number of countries of the world have recently had totalitarian regimes forced upon them against their will. The Government of the United States has made frequent protests against coercion and intimidation, in violation of the Yalta agreement, in Poland, Rumania, and Bulgaria. I must also state that in a number of other countries there have been similar developments.

At the present moment in world history nearly every nation must choose between alternative ways of life. The choice is too often not a free one.

One way of life is based upon the will of the majority, and is distinguished by free institutions, representative government, free elections, guaranties of individual liberty, freedom of speech and religion, and freedom from political oppression.

The second way of life is based upon the will of a minority forcibly imposed upon the majority. It relies upon terror and oppression, a controlled press and radio, fixed elections, and the suppression of personal freedoms.

I believe that it must be the policy of the United States to support free peoples who are resisting attempted subjugation by armed minorities or by outside pressures.

I believe that we must assist free peoples to work out their own destinies in their own way.

I believe that our help should be primarily through economic and financial aid which is essential to economic stability and orderly political processes.

The world is not static, and the *status quo* is not sacred. But we cannot allow changes in the *status quo* in violation of the

Charter of the United Nations by such methods as coercion, or by such subterfuges as political infiltration. In helping free and independent nations to maintain their freedom, the United States will be giving effect to the principles of the Charter of the United Nations.

It is necessary only to glance at a map to realize that the survival and integrity of the Greek nation are of grave importance in a much wider situation. If Greece should fall under the control of an armed minority, the effect upon its neighbor, Turkey, would be immediate and serious. Confusion and disorder might well spread throughout the entire Middle East.

Moreover, the disappearance of Greece as an independent state would have a profound effect upon those countries in Europe whose peoples are struggling against great difficulties to maintain their freedoms and their independence while they repair the damages of war.

It would be an unspeakable tragedy if these countries, which have struggled so long against overwhelming odds, should lose that victory for which they sacrificed so much. Collapse of free institutions and loss of independence would be disastrous not only for them but for the world. Discouragement and possibly failure would quickly be the lot of neighboring peoples striving to maintain their freedom and independence.

Should we fail to aid Greece and Turkey in this fateful hour, the effect will be far-reaching to the West as well as to the East.

We must take immediate and resolute action.

I therefore ask the Congress to provide authority for assistance to Greece and Turkey in the amount of $400,000,000 for the period ending June 30, 1948. In requesting these funds, I have taken into consideration the maximum amount of relief assistance which would be furnished to Greece out of the $350,000,000 which I recently requested that the Congress authorize for the prevention of starvation and suffering in countries devastated by the war.

In addition to funds, I ask the Congress to authorize the detail of American civilian and military personnel to Greece and Turkey, at the request of those countries, to assist in the tasks of reconstruction, and for the purpose of supervising the use of such financial and material assistance as may be furnished. I recommend that authority also be provided for the instruction and training of selected Greek and Turkish personnel.

Finally, I ask that the Congress provide authority which will permit the speediest and most effective use, in terms of needed commodities, supplies, and equipment, of such funds as may be authorized.

If further funds, or further authority, should be needed for purposes indicated in this message, I shall not hesitate to bring the situation before the Congress. On this subject the Executive and Legislative branches of the Government must work together.

This is a serious course upon which we embark. I would not recommend it except that the alternative is much more serious.

The United States contributed $341,000,000,000 toward winning World War II. This is an investment in world freedom and world peace.

The assistance that I am recommending for Greece and Turkey amounts to little more than one tenth of one percent of this investment. It is only common sense that we should safeguard this investment and make sure that it was not in vain.

The seeds of totalitarian regimes are nurtured by misery and want. They spread and grow in the evil soil of poverty and strife. They reach their full growth when the hope of a people for a better life has died.

We must keep that hope alive.

The free peoples of the world look to us for support in maintaining their freedoms.

If we falter in our leadership, we may endanger the peace of the world—and we shall surely endanger the welfare of our own Nation.

Great responsibilities have been placed upon us by the swift movement of events.

I am confident that the Congress will face these responsibilities squarely.

23 / GEORGE F. KENNAN ADVOCATES CONTAINMENT

In a series of memoranda prepared in 1946, and in an unsigned article appearing in Foreign Affairs, *George F. Kennan (1904–   ), American chargé d'affaires in Moscow, counselor in the State Department, and, later, Ambassador to Russia, developed the long-term containment policy which became the basis for America's foreign-relations posture during the Cold War. In a sense, it was the first clearly defined and systematically executed foreign policy of the United States.*

. . . Soviet diplomacy [is] at once easier and more difficult to deal with than the diplomacy of individual aggressive leaders like Napoleon and Hitler. On the one hand it is more sensitive to contrary force, more ready to yield on individual sectors of the diplomatic front when that force is felt to be too strong, and thus more rational in the logic and rhetoric of power. On the other hand it cannot be easily defeated or discouraged by a single victory on the part of its opponents. And the patient persistence by which it is animated means that it can be effectively countered not by sporadic acts which represent the momentary whims of democratic opinion but only by intelligent long-range policies on the part of Russia's adversaries—policies no less steady in their purpose, and no less variegated and resourceful in their application, than those of the Soviet Union itself.

In these circumstances it is clear that the main element of

SOURCE: "The Sources of Soviet Conduct," *Foreign Affairs*, XXV (July 1947), 566–82. Copyrighted by the Council on Foreign Relations, Inc., New York. Reprinted with permission.

any United States policy toward the Soviet Union must be that of a long-term, patient but firm and vigilant containment of Russian expansive tendencies. It is important to note, however, that such a policy has nothing to do with outward histrionics: with threats or blustering or superfluous gestures of outward "toughness." While the Kremlin is basically flexible in its reaction to political realities, it is by no means unamenable to considerations of prestige. Like almost any other government, it can be placed by tactless and threatening gestures in a position where it cannot afford to yield even though this might be dictated by its sense of realism. The Russian leaders are keen judges of human psychology, and as such they are highly conscious that loss of temper and of self-control is never a source of strength in political affairs. They are quick to exploit such evidences of weakness. For these reasons, it is a *sine qua non* of successful dealing with Russia that the foreign government in question should remain at all times cool and collected and that its demands on Russian policy should be put forward in such a manner as to leave the way open for a compliance not too detrimental to Russian prestige. . . .

It is clear that the United States cannot expect in the foreseeable future to enjoy political intimacy with the Soviet regime. It must continue to regard the Soviet Union as a rival, not a partner, in the political arena. It must continue to expect that Soviet policies will reflect no abstract love of peace and stability, no real faith in the possibility of a permanent happy coexistence of the Socialist and capitalist worlds, but rather a cautious, persistent pressure toward the disruption and weakening of all rival influence and rival power.

Balanced against this are the facts that Russia, as opposed to the western world in general, is still by far the weaker party, that Soviet policy is highly flexible, and that the Soviet society may well contain deficiencies which will eventually weaken its own total potential. This would of itself warrant the United States entering with reasonable confidence upon a policy of firm containment, designed to confront the Russians with unalterable counterforce at every point where they show signs of encroaching upon the interests of a peaceful and stable world.

But in actuality the possibilities for American policy are by no means limited to holding the line and hoping for the best. It is entirely possible for the United States to influence by its actions the internal developments, both within Russia and throughout the international Communist movement, by which Russian policy is largely determined. This is not only a question of the modest measure of informational activity which this government can conduct in the Soviet Union and elsewhere, although that, too, is important. It is rather a question of the degree to which the United States can create among the peoples of the world generally the impression of a country which knows what it wants, which is coping successfully with the problems of its internal life and with the responsibilities of a World Power, and which has a spiritual vitality capable of holding its own among the major ideological currents of the time. To the extent that such an impression can be created and maintained, the aims of Russian Communism must appear sterile and quixotic, the hopes and enthusiasm of Moscow's supporters must wane, and added strain must be imposed on the Kremlin's foreign policies. For the palsied decrepitude of the capitalist world is the keystone of Communist philosophy. Even the failure of the United States to experience the early economic depression which the ravens of the Red Square have been predicting with such complacent confidence since hostilities ceased would have deep and important repercussions throughout the Communist world.

By the same token, exhibitions of indecision, disunity and internal disintegration within this country have an exhilarating effect on the whole Communist movement. At each evidence of these tendencies, a thrill of hope and excitement goes through the Communist world; a new jauntiness can be noted in the Moscow tread; new groups of foreign supporters climb on to what they can only view as the band wagon of international politics; and Russian pressure increases all along the line in international affairs.

It would be an exaggeration to say that American behavior unassisted and alone could exercise a power of life and death over the Communist movement and bring about the early fall of Soviet power in Russia. But the United States has it in its power to increase enormously the strains under which Soviet policy must operate, to force upon the Kremlin a far greater degree of moderation and circumspection than it has had to observe in recent years, and in this way to promote tendencies which must eventually find their outlet in either the break-up or the gradual mellowing of Soviet power. For no mystical, Messianic movement—and particularly not that of the Kremlin—can face frustration indefinitely without eventually adjusting itself in one way or another to the logic of that state of affairs.

Thus the decision will really fall in large measure in this country itself. The issue of Soviet-American relations is in essence a test of the over-all worth of the United States as a nation among nations. To avoid destruction the United States need only measure up to its own best traditions and prove itself worthy of preservation as a great nation.

Surely, there was never a fairer test of national quality than this. In the light of these circumstances, the thoughtful observer of Russian-American relations will find no cause for complaint in the Kremlin's challenge to American society. He will rather experience a certain gratitude to a Providence which, by providing the American people with this implacable challenge, has made their entire security as a nation dependent on their pulling themselves together and accepting the responsibilities of moral and political leadership that history plainly intended them to bear.

24 / SECRETARY OF STATE ACHESON TAKES A STAND IN EUROPE AND ASIA

One of the major effects of the Cold War was to orient American foreign policy increasingly toward Europe. Secretary of State Dean Acheson's (1893–   ) speech of March 18, 1949, indicated this country's complete commitment to the North Atlantic Treaty Organization, a military alliance for the defense of Western Europe. In his speech of January 12, 1950, he made a much more limited commitment to the defense of the Far East. The speech probably encouraged the Soviet attempt to escape containment by advancing in Korea.

The Atlantic pact is a collective self-defense arrangement among the countries of the North Atlantic area. It is aimed at coordinating the exercise of the right of self-defense specifically recognized in article 51 of the United Nations Charter. It is designed to fit precisely into the framework of the United Nations and to assure practical measures for maintaining peace and security in harmony with the Charter. . . .

. . . We have learned our history lesson from two world wars in less than half a century. That experience has taught us that the control of Europe by a single aggressive, unfriendly power would constitute an intolerable threat to the national security of the United States. We participated in those two great wars to preserve the integrity and independence of the European half of the Atlantic community in order to preserve the integrity and independence of the American half. It is a simple fact,

SOURCE: *Department of State Bulletin,* XX (March 27, 1949), 384–88; XXII (January 23, 1950), 111–19.

proved by experience, that an outside attack on one member of this community is an attack upon all members.

We have also learned that if the free nations do not stand together, they will fall one by one. The stratagem of the aggressor is to keep his intended victims divided, or, better still, set them to quarreling among themselves. Then they can be picked off one by one without arousing unified resistance. We and the free nations of Europe are determined that history shall not repeat itself in that melancholy particular. . . .

In the compact world of today, the security of the United States cannot be defined in terms of boundaries and frontiers. A serious threat to international peace and security anywhere in the world is of direct concern to this country. Therefore it is our policy to help free peoples to maintain their integrity and independence, not only in Western Europe or in the Americas, but wherever the aid we are able to provide can be effective. Our actions in supporting the integrity and independence of Greece, Turkey, and Iran are expressions of that determination. Our interest in the security of these countries has been made clear, and we shall continue to pursue that policy.

In providing military assistance to other countries, both inside and outside the North Atlantic pact, we will give clear priority to the requirements for economic recovery. We will carefully balance the military assistance program with the capacity and requirements of the total economy, both at home and abroad.

But to return to the treaty, article 5 deals with the possibility, which unhappily cannot be excluded, that the nations joining together in the pact may have to face the eventuality of an armed attack. In this article, they agree that an armed attack on any of them, in Europe or North America, will be considered an attack on all of them. In the event of such an attack, each of them will take, individually and in concert with the other parties, whatever action it deems necessary to restore and maintain the security of the North Atlantic area, including the use of armed force. . . .

. . . Any measures for self-defense taken under the treaty will be reported to the Security Council of the United Nations.

These measures will continue only until the Security Council, with its primary responsibility, takes the necessary action to restore peace and maintain security. . . .

Too often peace has been thought of as a negative condition —the mere absence of war. We know now that we cannot achieve peace by taking a negative attitude. Peace is positive, and it has to be waged with all our thought, energy and courage, and with the conviction that war is not inevitable.

Under the leadership of President Truman, the United States is waging peace with a vigor and on a scale without precedent. While the war was being fought, this country took the initiative in the organization of the United Nations and related agencies for the collective and cooperative conduct of international affairs. We withdrew our military forces, except those required for occupation duties, and quickly reduced our military establishment to about one-tenth its wartime size. We contributed generously to postwar relief and rehabilitation.

When events called for firmness as well as generosity the United States waged peace by pledging its aid to free nations threatened by aggression and took prompt and vigorous action to fulfil that pledge. We have actively sought and are actively seeking to make the United Nations an effective instrument of international cooperation. We proposed, and with the eager cooperation of 16 other nations put into effect, a great concerted program for the economic recovery and spiritual reinvigoration of Europe. We joined the other American republics and we now join with Western Europe in treaties to strengthen the United Nations and insure international peace and security. . . .

A secure and stable peace is not a goal we can reach all at once and for all time. It is a dynamic state, produced by effort and faith, with justice and courage. The struggle is continuous and hard. The prize is never irrevocably ours.

To have this genuine peace we must constantly work for it. But we must do even more. We must make it clear that armed attack will be met by collective defense, prompt and effective.

That is the meaning of the North Atlantic pact.

. . . . .

What is the situation in regard to the military security of the Pacific area, and what is our policy in regard to it?

In the first place, the defeat and the disarmament of Japan has placed upon the United States the necessity of assuming the military defense of Japan so long as that is required, both in the interest of our security and in the interests of the security of the entire Pacific area and, in all honor, in the interest of Japanese security. We have American—and there are Australian—troops in Japan. I am not in a position to speak for the Australians, but I can assure you that there is no intention of any sort of abandoning or weakening the defenses of Japan and that whatever arrangements are to be made either through permanent settlement or otherwise, that defense must and shall be maintained.

This defensive perimeter runs along the Aleutians to Japan and then goes to the Ryukyus. We hold important defense positions in the Ryukyu Islands, and those we will continue to hold. In the interest of the population of the Ryukyu Islands, we will at an appropriate time offer to hold these islands under trusteeship of the United Nations. But they are essential parts of the defensive perimeter of the Pacific, and they must and will be held.

The defensive perimeter runs from the Ryukyus to the Philippine Islands. Our relations, our defensive relations with the Philippines are contained in agreements between us. Those agreements are being loyally carried out and will be loyally carried out. . . .

So far as the military security of other areas in the Pacific is concerned, it must be clear that no person can guarantee these areas against military attack. But it must also be clear that such a guarantee is hardly sensible or necessary within the realm of practical relationship.

Should such an attack occur—one hesitates to say where such an armed attack could come from—the initial reliance must be on the people attacked to resist it and then upon the commitments of the entire civilized world under the Charter of the United Nations which so far has not proved a weak reed to lean on by any people who are determined to protect their independence against outside aggression. But it is a mistake, I think, in considering Pacific and Far Eastern problems to become obsessed with military considerations. Important as they are, there are other problems that press, and these other problems are not capable of solution through military means. These other problems arise out of the susceptibility of many areas, and many countries in the Pacific area, to subversion and penetration. That cannot be stopped by military means.

The susceptibility to penetration arises because in many areas there are new governments which have little experience in governmental administration and have not become firmly established or perhaps firmly accepted in their countries. They grow, in part, from very serious economic problems, some of them growing out directly from the last war, others growing indirectly out of the last war because of the disruptions of trade with other parts of the world, with the disruption of arrangements which furnished credit and management to these areas for many years. That has resulted in dislocation of economic effort and in a good deal of suffering among the peoples concerned. In part this susceptibility to penetration comes from the great social upheaval about which I have been speaking, an upheaval which was carried on and confused a great deal by the Japanese occupation and by the propaganda which has gone on from Soviet sources since the war.

Here, then, are the problems in these other areas which require some policy on our part, and I should like to point out two facts to you and then discuss in more detail some of these areas.

The first fact is the great difference between our responsibility and our opportunities in the northern part of the Pacific area and in the southern part of the Pacific area. In the north, we have direct responsibility in Japan and we have direct opportunity to act. The same thing to a lesser degree is true in Korea. . . .

In the southerly part of the area, we are one of many nations who can do no more than help. The direct responsibility lies with the peoples concerned. . . .

That leads me to the other thing that I wanted to point out, and that is the limitation of effective American assistance. American assistance can be effective when it is the missing component in a situation which might otherwise be solved. The United States cannot furnish all these components to solve the question. It can not furnish determination, it can not furnish the will, and it can not furnish the loyalty of a people to its government. But if the will and if the determination exists and if the people are behind their government, then, and not always then, is there a very good chance. In that situation, American help can be effective and it can lead to an accomplishment which could not otherwise be achieved. . . .

So after this survey, what we conclude, I believe, is that there is a new day which has dawned in Asia. It is a day in which the Asian peoples are on their own, and know it, and intend to continue on their own. . . . We are their friends. We and those others are willing to help, but we can help only where we are wanted and only where the conditions of help are really sensible and possible.

25 / FORMER AMBASSADOR KENNEDY

FAVORS WITHDRAWAL

The increasing international commitment of the United States and the dangers of this commitment which were demonstrated by the Korean War brought on a flurry of neo-isolationism in 1951–52. In a speech delivered at the Law School Forum of the University of Virginia, the former Ambassador to Great Britain, Joseph P. Kennedy (1888–), called American policy politically and morally bankrupt and urged withdrawal from Korea, Berlin, and Europe in general.

As far back as March 18, 1946, I set forth in *Life* magazine what I considered should be the fundamentals of American policy. The first and foremost of these was that we should make and keep ourselves strong. Fundamental to any successful dealing with the world, was the maintenance here in the United States of a high standard of living. Whatever concrete actions might be suggested, to bankrupt this nation in the pursuit of them would mean our self-destruction. . . .

I naturally opposed Communism but I said if portions of Europe or Asia wish to go Communistic or even have Communism thrust upon them, we cannot stop it. Instead we must make sure of our strength and be certain not to fritter it away in battles that could not be won.

But where are we now? Beginning with intervention in the Italian elections and financial and political aid to Greece and Turkey, we have expanded our political and financial programs on an almost unbelievably wide scale. Billions have been spent in the Marshall plan, further billions in the occupation of Berlin, Western Germany and Japan. Military aid has been poured into Greece, Turkey, Iran, the nations of the North Atlantic Pact, French Indo-China, and now in Korea we are fighting the fourth greatest war in our history.

What have we in return for this effort? Friends? We have far fewer friends than we had in 1945. In Europe they are still asking for our dollars but what kind of friendship have we bought there? Is Western Europe determined to preserve for itself those ideals of democracy that we have been preaching? Put to the test now as to whether she will arm herself effectively, even with our aid, to deal with the Russian threat, is she showing the kind of determination and the kind of will that amounts to anything? Plans for economic unification have fallen apart in the light of nationalistic differences. French military power is only a shadow of its former self, and a strong minority of Communist sympathizers keeps France in endless political turmoil. The military strength of Britain is one-fourth of what

SOURCE: *Vital Speeches of the Day*, XVII (January 1951), 170–73. Reprinted with permission.

it was in 1946 and she shows every inclination to avoid the heavy burdens that would be involved in rebuilding it. West Germany, to date, has revealed no disposition to develop effective military strength. Italy is hopelessly ineffective and Greece can hardly police her own small territory. Where is there in all Europe any buffer against a massed Russian onslaught? Worse than this, where is there any determination to create such a buffer?

In the Middle East we have oil but no friends. Iran, Pakistan, even Egypt, seek neither our protection nor our influence. In Asia, China whose friendship with us seemed deep-seated and enduring, is now massed against us with men, powerful armies and new vengeful hatreds. Indonesia, Malay, Indo-China, are in revolt or heavy with discontent at the influences we represent. India is showing signs of succumbing to influences other than ours, more indigenous and more palatable to her desires. In Korea we are spending thousands of American lives to accomplish some unknown objective. Assume we stop the Reds somewhere across the belt of that peninsula, are we to continue fighting there indefinitely?

On the other side of the Iron Curtain are massed manpower and military strength of a type that the world has never seen. . . .

To engage these vast armies on the European or the Asian continent is foolhardy, but that is the direction towards which our policy has been tending.

That policy is suicidal. It has made us no foul weather friends. It has kept our armament scattered over the globe. It has picked one battlefield and threatens to pick others impossibly removed from our sources of supply. It has not contained Communism. By our methods of opposition it has solidified Communism, where otherwise Communism might have bred within itself internal dissensions. Our policy today is politically and morally a bankrupt policy.

I can see no alternative other than having the courage to wash up this policy and start with the fundamentals I urged more than five years ago. It is absurd to believe that the United Nations can lead us out of this situation. The veto power alone makes it a hopeless instrumentality for world peace. The unwillingness of half the world to want world peace makes impossible effective organization to impose any such peace. In short, our chief source of reliance must be ourselves and we cannot sacrifice ourselves to save those who do not seem to wish to save themselves.

A first step in the pursuit of this policy is to get out of Korea —indeed, to get out of every point in Asia which we do not plan realistically to hold in our own defense. Such a policy means that in the Pacific we will pick our own battlegrounds if we are forced to fight and not have them determined by political and ideological considerations that have no relationship to our own defense.

The next step in pursuit of this policy is to apply the same principle to Europe. Today it is idle to talk of being able to hold the line of the Elbe or the line of the Rhine. Why should we waste valuable resources in making such an attempt? If the weakened European nations wish to hold that line and demonstrate a determination to do so, it may be that we can afford them some help. But to put arms and men into a Quixotic military adventure makes no sense whatever. What have we gained by staying in Berlin? Everyone knows we can be pushed out the moment the Russians choose to push us out. Isn't it better to get out now and use the resources, that would otherwise be sacrificed, at a point that counts?

The billions that we have squandered on these enterprises could have been far more effectively used in this hemisphere and on the seas that surround it. Had we the defenses in Iceland today that one-hundredth of the money spent in Berlin could have built, we would have purchased safety with our money rather than added danger. We need defenses in this hemisphere, in Canada, in the Caribbean and in Latin America. After all, these are our neighbors whose security is inevitably tied up with our own. We have no reason to believe that cooperation on their part will not be forthcoming and we can, and should insist upon it.

People will say, however, that this policy will not contain Communism. Will our present policy do so? Can we possibly contain Communist Russia, if she chooses to march, by a far flung battle line in the middle of Europe? The truth is that our only real hope is to keep Russia, if she chooses to march, on the other side of the Atlantic and make Communism much too costly for her to try to cross the seas. It may be that Europe for a decade or a generation or more will turn Communistic. But in doing so, it may break of itself as a unified force. Communism still has to prove itself to its peoples as a government that will achieve for them a better way of living. The more people that it will have to govern, the more necessary it becomes for those who govern to justify themselves to those being governed. The more peoples that are under its yoke, the greater are the possibilities of revolt. Moreover, it seems certain that Communism spread over Europe will not rest content with being governed by a handful of men in the Kremlin. French or Italian Communists will soon develop splinter organizations that will destroy the singleness that today characterizes Russian Communism. Tito in Jugoslavia is already demonstrating this fact. Mao in China is not likely to take his orders too long from Stalin, especially when the only non-Asiatics left upon Asiatic soil to fight are the Russians.

This policy will, of course, be criticized as appeasement. No word is more mistakenly used. Is it appeasement to withdraw from unwise commitments, to arm yourself to the teeth and to make clear just exactly how and for what you will fight? If it is wise in our interest not to make commitments that endanger our security, and this is appeasement, then I am for appeasement. I can recall only too well the precious time bought by Chamberlain at Munich. I applauded that purchase then; I would applaud it today. Today, however, while we have avoided a Munich we are coming perilously close to another Dunkirk. Personally, I should choose to escape the latter. . . .

An attitude of realism such as this is, I submit, in accord with our historic traditions. We have never wanted a part of other peoples' scrapes. Today we have them and just why, nobody quite seems to know. What business is it of ours to support French colonial policy in Indo-China or to achieve Mr. Syngman Rhee's concepts of democracy in Korea? Shall we now send the marines into the mountains of Tibet to keep the Dalai Lama on his throne? We can do well to mind our business and interfere only where somebody threatens our business and our homes. . . .

An Atlas, whose back is bowed and whose hands are busy holding up the world, has no arms to lift to deal with his own defense. Increase his burdens and you will crush him, or attack him from behind and he cannot turn. This is our present posture. It strangles our might. The suggestions I make would unleash our strength. They would, I am sure, give considerable pause to the strategists and planners of the Kremlin. They would—and I count this most—conserve American lives for American ends, not waste them in the freezing hills of Korea or on the battle-scarred plains of Western Germany.

26 / SECRETARY OF STATE DULLES CONSIDERS LIBERATION AND MASSIVE RETALIATION

The containment policy, while effective, did not seem to offer any opportunity for victory in the Cold War. Even before his appointment as Secretary of State, John Foster Dulles (1888–1959) had suggested the more dynamic alternative of "liberating" the peoples under the domination of the Soviet Union. He explained this concept to the Foreign Relations Committee on January 15, 1953. On March 19 and April 14, 1954, he amplified before the same committee an earlier speech in which he had suggested the reliance on means of massive retaliation in place of the more complicated and costly system of, in effect, establishing American garrisons around the perimeter of the Communist bloc. In both cases, he articulated an essentially Europe-oriented foreign policy.

The CHAIRMAN [*Senator Wiley*]. I am particularly interested in something I read recently, to the effect that you stated you were not in favor of the policy of containment. I think you advocated a more dynamic or positive policy.

Can you tell us more specifically what you have in mind? . . .

Mr. DULLES. There are a number of policy matters which I would prefer to discuss with the committee in executive session, but I have no objection to saying in open session what I have said before: namely, that we shall never have a secure peace or a happy world so long as Soviet communism dominates one-third of all of the peoples that there are, and is in the process of trying at least to extend its rule to many others.

These people who are enslaved are people who deserve to be free, and who, from our own selfish standpoint, ought to be free because if they are the servile instruments of aggressive despotism, they will eventually be welded into a force which will be highly dangerous to ourselves and to all of the free world.

Therefore, we must always have in mind the liberation of these captive peoples. Now, liberation does not mean a war of liberation. Liberation can be accomplished by processes short of war. We have, as one example, not an ideal example, but it illustrates my point, the defection of Yugoslavia, under Tito from the domination of Soviet communism.

Well, that rule of Tito is not one which we admire, and it has many aspects of despotism, itself; but at least it illustrates that it is possible to disintegrate this present monolithic structure which, as I say, represents approximately one-third of all the people that there are in the world.

The present tie between China and Moscow is an unholy arrangement which is contrary to the traditions, the hopes, the aspirations of the Chinese people. Certainly we cannot tolerate a continuance of that, or a welding of the 450 million people of China into the servile instruments of Soviet aggression.

SOURCE: *Nomination of John Foster Dulles,* Hearings before the Foreign Relations Committee, U.S. Senate, 83d Cong., 1st sess. (Washington, 1953); *Statement of Secretary of State John Foster Dulles . . . on Foreign Policy and Its Relation to Military Programs,* Hearings before the Foreign Relations Committee, U.S. Senate, 83d Cong., 2d sess. (Washington, 1954).

Therefore, a policy which only aims at containing Russia where it now is, is, in itself, an unsound policy; but it is a policy which is bound to fail because a purely defensive policy never wins against an aggressive policy. If our only policy is to stay where we are, we will be driven back. It is only by keeping alive the hope of liberation, by taking advantage of that wherever opportunity arises, that we will end this terrible peril which dominates the world, which imposes upon us such terrible sacrifices and so great fears for the future. But all of this can be done and must be done in ways which will not provoke a general war, or in ways which will not provoke an insurrection which would be crushed with bloody violence, such as was the case, for example, when the Russians instigated the Polish revolt, under General Bor, and merely sat by and watched them when the Germans exterminated those who were revolting. . . .

Senator SMITH of New Jersey. . . . Now, Mr. Dulles, the question has been raised in some quarters as to whether you are more interested in one part of the world than in others. On the other hand, I have understood you to take the position of the global nature of present world affairs, rather than particular emphasis on any one area.

Will you give us your thought on that?

Mr. DULLES. In my opinion, under the modern conditions, both of open warfare and, you might call it, political warfare, there is no geographical area which is effectively defensible without regard to the other. In other words, a condition of interdependence has been forced upon us by modern conditions, and the use to which modern facilities are put by the Soviet Communists.

There are those in Europe, for example, who believe or seem to believe that Europe alone could be made defensible; just as there are people who believe that the United States alone can be made defensible.

We call those people a name, I never liked the use of such names, because they lend themselves to misinterpretation and unfair use, but such people have been called isolationists.

I say, the people in Europe who believe that Europe alone can be defensible, without regard to what happens in Asia and

Africa, they are even more blind than those who believe that our own country can be made defensible without regard to what goes on anywhere else.

Now, the Soviet Communist strategy is global, and to the extent that we give priority to any area, it can only be because the strategy of a global conspiracy requires us to do so. . . .

Secretary DULLES. . . . . The menace of Soviet bloc despotism, which now holds in its grip one-third of the world's peoples, presents the most serious danger that has ever confronted us. The main aspects of this threat are apparent.

First, the Soviet rulers seem to feel secure only in a world of conformity dominated by them. Partly, no doubt, they are driven by lust for power. But, to a considerable extent, I believe, they are driven by fear of freedom. To them freedom is a threat to be stamped out wherever it approaches their world.

In the second place, the Soviet bloc possesses what is in many ways the most formidable military establishment the world has ever known. Its great strength is manpower, but also it is strong in terms of planes, submarines, and atomic capabilities. This vast empire dominates the central Eurasian land mass extending from the River Elbe in Germany to the Pacific. From within an orbit of 20,000 miles, it could strike by land at any one of approximately 20 states of Europe, the Middle East and Asia, and by air it could strike the North American Continent.

Nor is the threat only military. The Soviet bloc also commands a political apparatus which operates in every country of the world, seeking to capitalize upon all of the discontents and unsatisfied ambitions which inevitably exist in greater or less degree throughout the free world.

In the fourth place, the threat is virtually unlimited so far as time is concerned. Soviet communism operates not in terms of an individual lifetime so that the threat will end with someone's death. It operates in terms of what Lenin and Stalin called "an entire historical era."

To meet the military threat requires on our side a strategy which is both well-conceived and well-implemented. This military defense must be within the capacity of the free world to sustain it for an indefinite time without such impairment of its economic and social fabric as would expose it to piecemeal seizure from within by the political apparatus of communism.

This calls for thinking and planning which is imaginative; which takes maximum possible advantage of the special resources of the free nations; and which is steadily developed and adapted to changing conditions. The fundamental aim of our national security policies is to deter aggression and thereby avert a new war. The essentials of this problem may be briefly summarized as follows:

First, the free nations can achieve security only by a collective system of defense. No single nation can develop alone adequate power to deter Soviet-bloc aggression against its vital interests. By providing joint facilities and by combining their resources, the free nations can achieve a total strength and a flexibility which can surpass that of any potential enemy and can do so at bearable cost.

This collective-security concept is the most highly developed in the North Atlantic Treaty Organization. But it [is] also embodied in the Rio Pact of 1947 and, in more limited form, in various security arrangements in the Far East. The Turkey-Pakistan agreement marks the beginning of applying the collective-security concept in the Middle East. The United Nations is moving in the same direction, as shown by its "Uniting for Peace" Resolution of 1951.

Secondly, in organizing their collective defense, the free nations should not attempt to match the Soviet bloc man for man and gun for gun. The best way to deter aggression is to make the aggressor know in advance that he will suffer damage outweighing what he can hope to gain. Thus an aggressor must not be able to count upon a sanctuary status for those resources which he does not use in committing aggression.

To apply this deterrent principle the free world must maintain and be prepared to use effective means to make aggression too costly to be tempting.

It must have the mobility and flexibility to bring collective power to bear against an enemy on a selective or massive basis as conditions may require. For this purpose its arsenal must include a wide range of air, sea, and land power based on both conventional and atomic weapons. These new weapons can be used not only for strategic purposes but also for tactical purposes. The greatest deterrent to war is the ability of the free world to respond by means best suited to the particular area and circumstances. There should be a capacity—I emphasize the word "capacity"—for massive retaliation without delay. I point out that the possession of that capacity does not impose the necessity of using it in every instance of attack. It is not our intention to turn every local war into a general war.

The magnitude and duration of the present danger and the need for flexibility of means to deter that danger makes it vital to the United States, as never before, that it have firm allies. A firm alliance depends not merely upon documents, although these may be important. There must also be trust, understanding, and good will as between the free nations. This implies not merely military commitments, but good economic and cultural relations as well. It is not charity on the part of the United States to be concerned with the economic health of other nations which help to support the basic strategy which I describe. Neither is their good will, or the lack of it, a matter to which we can be indifferent. All of this means that foreign policy has assumed, as never before, a vital importance for the security of the United States. . . .

Senator GILLETTE. . . . First, I want to ask you this: In all of this discussion, neither in your statement nor in any question asked here nor in any answer that has been given has there been the remotest reference to the United Nations organization and its utilization for the purposes that have been set up. Do you wish to comment on why that has not been done?

Secretary DULLES. My opening statement did refer to the United Nations, Senator Gillette; . . .

Senator GILLETTE. There is no intention then, on your part or on the part of the present Government, the executive department, to abandon the United Nations as an instrumentality set up for the purpose its sponsors hoped it would accomplish?

Secretary DULLES. Not at all. I would certainly—there was not the slightest thought of abandoning the United Nations, and

I think that probably the fact that President Eisenhower went to the United Nations General Assembly to deliver his historic address on the turning of atomic forces of life rather than of death, the fact that he went to the United Nations to make that, has done more to give a lift and fresh inspiration to the United Nations than anything that has happened for quite a long time. . . .

We have had to adopt certain expedients to meet the excessive and abusive use of the veto power in the Security Council by the Soviet Union; but, subject to the necessary adaptation to that practical situation, there is every desire and intention on the part of the administration to work closely with and to strengthen in every feasible way the United Nations.

PART VI

The United States in the Contemporary World

(1959–1965)

THE very success of the containment policy, combined with the evidence of dissension within the Communist bloc presented by the Sino-Soviet rift, produced the demand for a still firmer, more militant policy in which the United States would seize the initiative (Selection 27). It also, however, renewed the possibility of a general detente in which the United Nations would play a leading role. Aware of the danger in assuming too militant a posture, President Eisenhower chose the latter course by urging the United Nations to take the responsibility for the establishment of an international police force, an international aid program for emergent nations, and world disarmament (Selection 28).

The failure of the United Nations to respond effectively to this call and the continuing development of new points of friction throughout the world led to a new and even stronger assertion of American leadership and to the high point of American commitment (Selection 29). But this was soon followed by the afterthought that the changing world situation required a more definite break with America's Cold War posture than President Kennedy's inaugural address suggested.

By 1964 the theory that the United States was overcommitted and in need of reassessing its entire foreign policy came to be voiced with increasing frequency (Selection 30). The fact that tensions in Europe had somewhat subsided, while at the same time American difficulties in the Caribbean and the Far East increased, lent weight to these arguments. The pace of events to which rapid reactions had to be forthcoming prevented more than a piecemeal change in policy, however. Faced by the strong possibility of the loss of South Vietnam and confronted, at the same time, by a revolution in the Dominican Republic which might have led to further Communist inroads in this hemisphere, President Johnson reasserted the essential features of the containment policy, directed this time not only against the Soviet Union, but even more particularly against China (Selection 31). He also moved to implement this policy through a massive American military commitment despite persistent criticism, both at home and abroad.

27 / EUGENE LYONS URGES AMERICA
TO CONFRONT THE ENEMY

The idea that the Cold War could be and ought to be won persisted in some circles long after it had been abandoned by the United State government. In a speech before the Detroit Economic Club on February 16, 1959, Eugene Lyons (1898–   ), senior editor of the Reader's Digest, *took the Administration to task for not assuming a more determined military posture and for yielding unnecessarily to Russian pressure. It should be the United States and not the Soviet Union, he insisted, which determined where and how future confrontations should occur.*

The Great Western Powers, custodians of mankind's treasures of freedom and culture, seem to have suffered a disastrous loss

SOURCE: *Vital Speeches of the Day,* XXV (March 1959), 357–61. Reprinted with permission.

of nerve. Western policies have been wholly defensive, impro-
vised in a panic to meet the crisis of the hour, while ignoring
the larger, all-embracing crisis of this historical period, of which
each new outbreak is only a part.

We have shied away from firm, consistent policies on the
ground that we might "antagonize" the enemy and close the
doors to "understandings" with him. But the enemy has had no
such inhibitions. He has attacked, attacked, and attacked. If you
are under any illusion that there has been a change on this
score since Stalin's death, read the speeches of Khrushchev and
Gromyko at their Party Congress last month.

Oh I know, I shall be asked, "Do you want a Third World
War?" But the question makes little sense. It evades the grim
lesson of very recent history—that appeasement and retreat, far
from ending danger are the guarantees of more terrible dangers
to come. Nobody in his senses wants war—and that includes me
and Khrushchev. The real question is whether war is best avoided
by softness, jitters, submission to blackmail, piecemeal surrenders
—or by a principled, self-respecting firmness.

Those who point with trembling fingers to the new military
strength of the Soviets should be reminded that communism
scored its greatest triumphs precisely in the years when the free
world held overwhelming military superiority; that the Kremlin
conquered country after country at a time when we had an
absolute monopoly of nuclear power. This land of poker players
has consistently been bluffed out of winning hands. . . .

There are those who argue that anything—even surrender—
is better than war. Others imply this without saying it. At best
that's a shabby, morally shocking proposition. People who fear
death more than they love liberty, justice, and honor no longer
deserve to survive as independent human beings. Already, before the chains have been welded on their wrists and ankles,
they have assumed the posture of slaves.

The mischief of announcing in advance that we don't intend
to defend our way of life is that it helps to provoke the very
catastrophe it proposes to evade. For it amounts to an open
invitation to the enemy to make more demands, issue more
daring ultimatums, create more dangerous crises. And these in

turn push the world closer and closer to the wall of ultimate despair where even a terrified kitten turns on a big dog.

The advocates of surrender-rather-than-war are still few, of course. But their extreme view reflects, as in an enlarging mirror, the attitude of the free world. It differs only in degree from the policies we have actually followed.

Take Korea. There we won a costly victory, then proceeded to turn it into a more costly defeat, rather than risk the attack on the enemy's sanctuary in Manchuria demanded by Mac-Arthur, Van Fleet, Stratmeyer [sic] and nearly all our military leaders. And remember that we had, at one time, unquestioned control of the air and exclusive control of the atomic weapon. Red China could not possibly have held out alone, and Moscow would not have courted annihilation.

A decisive United Nations victory might well have stopped Chinese Communism in its tracks and reversed the whole trend of Asian history. But instead of clinching our victory, we settled for an uneasy stalemate that will burst into flames again just as soon as Moscow and Peiping consider the time propitious.

Then there was the siege of Berlin. Of what avail was the air-lift to save the city, if we are called upon to save it again? In retrospect it is clear that had we followed the advice of the American military men closest to the scene—had we established our rights of access by force—there would have been no war, and there might have been no repetition of the challenge at a more dangerous time, such as we face today.

An even greater opportunity to arrest the expansion of communism—the kind that may not return for a great many years—was opened up when the people of Hungary overthrew their hated puppet regime. There were a hundred things the free world could have done, this side of open military involvement, to help the heroic people maintain their new-won freedom and head off Soviet intervention. Moscow, in fact, hesitated for nearly a week before sending its tanks rolling. It had to make sure that the West would not interfere with the slaughter. Obligingly, we gave them that assurance.

Yet the Kremlin was scarcely in a position then to invite a world war. Its whole satellite empire was tensed for revolt, and its own country, especially its youth, was in a rebellious mood. But Moscow had one great source of strength—namely, our psychological weakness. Again free nations were paralyzed by lack of nerve and heart and moral passion, and the unique chance to cut communism down to size was deliberately thrown away.

Or turn to China. In 1955 we forced the Nationalists to give up the Tachen Islands. Today we see that this has merely enabled the communists to advance their fighting line to Quemoy and Matsu.

When the aggression against Quemoy was unleashed, a few months ago, hysterical voices were raised here, in England, and elsewhere, demanding withdrawal from the offshore islands. They painted a panicky picture of the world going up in smoke unless the Chinese communists got what they wanted, and quick. But Secretary Dulles, almost alone, insisted on rejecting intimidation. And even limited resistance has sufficed to deny the communists another victory by default.

If those islands are surrendered, or lost, exactly nothing will be settled. The line of conflict will simply have been moved deeper into our area—to Formosa, then to Okinawa and other American outposts, and after that perhaps to the Philippines. The trouble with buying peace by concessions and compromise is that the communists never stay bought. On the contrary, every payment "ups the ante" for the next hold-up.

And today there are voices, not so many or so loud but still powerful, urging that we seek what they call a "sensible compromise" in Berlin. Their zeal for appeasement is masked with beguiling talk of negotiation and disengagement—but it's still the same sick urge to surrender rather than risk conflict. . . .

To stand fast involves risks, terrible risks. But the risks of yielding are far greater, far more terrible. Remember that the only threatened segments of the map which have been kept out of communist hands are those where we showed courage and a clear determination to back words with action. Greece and Iran and at least part of Turkey would by this time have been securely behind the Iron Curtain had we not acted boldly and in time.

By the same token, our position is least stable, most explosive, precisely in the areas where we made most concessions and surrenders, as in Germany and Korea and China. We sought to buy peace in our time by turning over 100 million people in Eastern Europe—all of them our friends and most of them our allies—to the Red barbarians. We sought to buy peace in Asia by giving communism the right of way in Manchuria, then in all of China. You know what we bought instead.

Much of our weakness derives from a myth that defies common sense—the enfeebling myth that Soviets somehow dread war less than we do; that if we dare affirm our rights they will begin tossing bombs. The men in the Kremlin are utterly ruthless, but they are not suicidal maniacs. They are more determined than ever to achieve one communist world, but this doesn't mean that they seek an all-out global war.

On the contrary, they aim to take over our world and its wealth intact, not in a heap of nuclear ruins. Above all, they don't want their own base of power, Soviet Russia, and the material foundations of that power, the Soviet industrial complex, reduced to rubble. They do not, of course, exclude the possibility of war, but they are profoundly sure that they can win the world without a major war, by means of the relentless harassments that we have come to call the cold war.

Now as always, the communists count on victory through propaganda, subversion, machiavellian diplomacy, the fomenting of economic crises and civil strife in target areas. They count on undermining our self-confidence and in the end destroying our will to resist. Safe in the knowledge that we won't start a final fight, they whip up panic fear of war in order to exact concessions, compromises and thinly disguised surrenders from a terrorized world. . . .

We have no alternative in common sense but to maintain our military vitality. It's our last-ditch insurance against all contingencies, the guarantee of everything else we do or dare. But the fateful decisions are being made now, by means short of war. The much discussed gap in missiles is negligible by comparison with the huge, almost complete gap in political weapons—those that have been giving the communists an unbroken series of large and small victories. That's the gap, above all, that must be closed if we are to survive. . . .

Like it or not, the great and inescapable task of our epoch is not to end the cold war but to win it. And to win it we must acknowledge its reality, then develop a strategy for fighting it boldly, aggressively, on a scale commensurate with the stakes involved—meanwhile maintaining military superiority to make sure that the war remains cold.

It's late, but not too late, to save our civilization and the values we cherish from being overrun by the new barbarism. We must face up, once and for all, to the fact that the struggle with communism can't be wished away; that it won't end until their world or ours is eliminated. There is no reason why we should merely wait for the next communist blow to descend. We, too, should confront the enemy with hard choices at times and in places of our choosing; encourage and intensify the tides of mutiny under the policed surface of Soviet life; keep the communists constantly off balance—in sum, we should do to them what they have been so successfully doing to us.

28 / PRESIDENT EISENHOWER BACKS
THE UNITED NATIONS

In his speech to the General Assembly of the United Nations on September 22, 1960, President Dwight D. Eisenhower (1890–) renewed the strong and sweeping commitment of the United States to international cooperation for peace. Rejecting the idea of a unilateral American victory in the Cold War and aware of the difficulties besetting the United Nations, he made the effort to revive that organization's effectiveness by giving the full endorsement of the United States to its activities.

Today I come before you because our human commonwealth is once again in a state of anxiety and turmoil. Urgent issues confront us.

The first proposition I place before you is that only through the United Nations Organization and its truly democratic processes can humanity make real and universal progress toward the goal of peace with justice. Therefore I believe that to support the United Nations Organization and its properly constituted mechanisms and its selected officers is the road of greatest promise in peaceful progress. To attempt to hinder or stultify the United Nations or to deprecate its importance is to contribute to world unrest and, indeed, to incite the crises that from time to time so disturb all men. The United States stands squarely and unequivocally in support of the United Nations and those acting under its mandate in the interest of peace.

Nowhere is the challenge to the international community and to peace and orderly progress more evident than in Africa, rich in human and natural resources and bright with promise. Recent events there have brought into being what is, in effect, a vast continent of newly independent nations.

Outside interference with these newly emerging nations, all eager to undertake the tasks of modernization, has created a serious challenge to the authority of the United Nations. . . .

In response to the call of the Republic of the Congo, the United Nations, under its outstanding Secretary-General, has recently mounted a large-scale effort to provide that new republic with help. That effort has been flagrantly attacked by a few nations which wish to prolong strife in the Congo for their own purposes. The criticism directed by these nations against the Secretary-General, who has honorably and effectively fulfilled the mandate which he received from the United Nations, is nothing less than a direct attack upon the United Nations itself. In my opinion, he, the Secretary-General, has earned the support and gratitude of every peace-loving nation.

The people of the Congo are entitled to build up their country in peace and freedom. Intervention by other nations in their

SOURCE: *Department of State Bulletin*, XLIII (October 10, 1960), 551–57.

internal affairs would deny them that right and create a focus of conflict in the heart of Africa.

The issue thus posed in the Congo could well arise elsewhere in Africa. The resolution of this issue will determine whether the United Nations is able to protect not only the new nations of Africa but also other countries against outside pressures. . . .

The changes which are occurring in Africa are also evident elsewhere. Indeed, Africa is but one part of the new world of change and progress which is emerging in all the developing areas.

We must carry forward and intensify our programs of assistance for the economic and social development in freedom of other areas, particularly in Latin America, Asia, and the Middle East.

Beyond this, we must never forget that there are hundreds of millions of people, particularly in the less developed parts of the world, suffering from hunger and malnutrition, even though a number of countries, my own included, are producing food in surplus. This paradox should not be allowed to continue.

The United States is already carrying out substantial programs to make its surpluses available to countries of greatest need. My country is also ready to join with other members of the United Nations in devising a workable scheme to provide food to member states through the United Nations system, relying on the advice and assistance of the Food and Agriculture Organization. . . .

In the developing areas we must seek to promote peaceful change, as well as to assist economic and social progress. To do this—to assist peaceful change—the international community must be able to manifest its presence in emergencies through United Nations observers or forces.

I should like to see member countries take positive action on the suggestions in the Secretary-General's report looking to the creation of a qualified staff within the Secretariat to assist him in meeting future needs for United Nations forces. Some progress has been made since that time. Much remains to be done.

The Secretary-General has now suggested that members should maintain a readiness to meet possible future requests from the United Nations for contributions to such forces. All countries represented here should respond to this need by ear-marking national contingents which could take part in United Nations forces in case of need.

The time to do it is now—at this Assembly.

I assure countries which now receive assistance from the United States that we favor use of the assistance to help them maintain such contingents in the state of readiness suggested by the Secretary-General. To assist the Secretary-General's ef-forts, the United States is prepared to earmark also substantial air and sea transport facilities on a standby basis to help move contingents requested by the United Nations in any future emergency.

Over the long run, further progress toward increasing the United Nations' ability to respond to future needs is surely pos-sible. The prospects for such progress, however, will remain just that—prospects—unless we move now to exploit the immediate possibilities for practical action suggested by the Secretary-General.

Another problem confronting us involves outer space.

The emergence of this new world poses a vital issue: Will outer space be preserved for peaceful use and developed for the benefit of all mankind? Or will it become another focus for the arms race—and thus an area of dangerous and sterile competi-tion?

The choice is urgent. And it is ours to make.

The nations of the world have recently united in declaring the continent of Antarctica "off limits" to military preparations. We could extend the principle to an even more important sphere. National vested interests have not yet been developed in space or in celestial bodies. Barriers to agreement are now lower than they will ever be again.

The opportunity may be fleeting. Before many years have passed, the point of no return may have passed. . . .

But armaments must also be controlled here on earth if civili-zation is to be assured of survival. These efforts must extend both to conventional and nonconventional armaments.

My country has made specific proposals to this end during the past year. New United States proposals were put forward on June 27, with the hope that they could serve as the basis for negotiations to achieve general disarmament. The United States still supports these proposals.

The Communist nations' walkout at Geneva, when they learned that we were about to submit these proposals, brought negotiations to an abrupt halt. Their unexplained action does not, however, reduce the urgent need for arms control.

My country believes that negotiations can—and should—soon be resumed. Our aim is to reach agreement on all the various measures that will bring general and complete disarmament. Any honest appraisal, however, must recognize that this is an immense task. It will take time.

We should not have to wait until we have agreed on all the detailed measures to reach this goal before we begin to move toward disarmament. Specific and promising steps to this end were suggested in our June 27 proposals.

If negotiations can be resumed, it may be possible to deal particularly with two pressing dangers—that of war by miscalculation and that of mounting nuclear weapons stockpiles. . . .

Men everywhere want to disarm. They want their wealth and labor to be spent not for war but for food, for clothing, for shelter, for medicine, for schools.

Time and again the American people have voiced this yearning—to join with men of good will everywhere in building a better world. We always stand ready to consider any feasible proposal to this end. And as I have said so many times the United States is always ready to negotiate with any country which in integrity and sincerity shows itself ready to talk about any of these problems. We ask only this—that such a program not give military advantage to any nation and that it permit men to inspect the disarmament of other nations.

A disarmament program which was not inspected and guaranteed would increase, not reduce, the risk of war.

The international control of atomic energy and general and complete disarmament can no more be accomplished by rhetoric than can the economic development of newly independent countries. Both of these immense tasks facing mankind call for serious, painstaking, costly, laborious, and nonpropaganda approaches. . . .

The basic fact today of all change in the domain of international affairs is the need to forge the bonds and build the structure of a true world community.

The United Nations is available to mankind to help it create just such a community. It has accomplished what no nation singly, or any limited group of nations, could have accomplished. It has become the forum of all peoples and the structure about which they can center their joint endeavors to create a better future for our world. . . .

The generating force behind a successful United Nations must be the noble idea that a true international community can build a peace with justice if only people will work together patiently in an atmosphere of open trust.

In urging progress toward a world community, I cite the American concept of the destiny of a progressive society. Here in this land, in what was once a wilderness, we have generated a society and a civilization drawn from many sources. Yet out of the mixture of many peoples and faiths we have developed unity in freedom—a unity designed to protect the rights of each individual while enhancing the freedom and well-being of all.

This concept of unity in freedom, drawn from the diversity of many racial strains and cultures, we would like to see made a reality for all mankind. This concept should apply within every nation as it does among nations. We believe that the right of every man to participate through his or her vote in self-government is as precious as the right of each nation here represented to vote its own convictions in this Assembly. I should like to see a universal plebiscite in which every individual in the world would be given the opportunity freely and secretly to answer this question: Do you want this right? Opposed to the idea of two hostile, embittered worlds in perpetual conflict, we envisage a single world community, as yet unrealized but advancing steadily toward fulfillment through our plans, our efforts, and our collective ideas.

Thus we see as our goal, not a superstate above nations, but a world community embracing them all, rooted in law and justice and enhancing the potentialities and common purposes of all peoples.

As we enter the decade of the 1960's, let us launch a renewed effort to strengthen this international community, to forge new bonds between its members in undertaking new ventures on behalf of all mankind.

As we take up this task, let us not delude ourselves that the absence of war alone is a sufficient basis for a peaceful world. I repeat, we must also build a world of justice under law, and we must overcome poverty, illiteracy, and disease.

We of the United States will join with you in making a mounting effort to build the structure of true peace—a peace in which all peoples may progress constantly to higher levels of human achievement. The means are at hand. We have but to use them with a wisdom and energy worthy of our cause.

29 / PRESIDENT KENNEDY ASSERTS AMERICA'S WORLD LEADERSHIP

The inaugural address of President John F. Kennedy (1917–1963) on January 20, 1961, was almost entirely devoted to foreign policy. Proudly and unequivocally, it announced America's acceptance of its role of world leadership. Implicit in it was the recognition that the Cold War had ended and that at least the possibility for the settlement of world problems now existed.

. . . Let the word go forth from this time and place, to friend and foe alike, that the torch has been passed to a new generation of Americans—born in this century, tempered by war, disciplined by a hard and bitter peace, proud of our ancient heritage—and

SOURCE: *Congressional Record*, 87th Cong., 1st sess. (1961), pp. 1012–13.

unwilling to witness or permit the slow undoing of those human rights to which this Nation has always been committed, and to which we are committed today at home and around the world.

Let every nation know, whether it wishes us well or ill, that we shall pay any price, bear any burden, meet any hardship, support any friend, oppose any foe, in order to assure the survival and the success of liberty.

This much we pledge—and more.

To those old allies whose cultural and spiritual origins we share, we pledge the loyalty of faithful friends. United, there is little we cannot do in a host of cooperative ventures. Divided, there is little we can do—for we dare not meet a powerful challenge at odds and split asunder.

To those new States whom we welcome to the ranks of the free, we pledge our word that one form of colonial control shall not have passed away merely to be replaced by a far more iron tyranny. We shall not always expect to find them supporting our view. But we shall always hope to find them strongly supporting their own freedom—and to remember that, in the past, those who foolishly sought power by riding the back of the tiger ended up inside.

To those peoples in the huts and villages of half the globe struggling to break the bonds of mass misery, we pledge our best efforts to help them help themselves, for whatever period is required—not because the Communists may be doing it, not because we seek their votes, but because it is right. If a free society cannot save the many who are poor, it cannot save the few who are rich.

To our sister republics south of our border, we offer a special pledge—to convert our good words into good deeds, in a new alliance for progress, to assist free men and free governments in casting off the chains of poverty. But this peaceful revolution of hope cannot become the prey of hostile powers. Let all our neighbors know that we shall join with them to oppose aggression or subversion anywhere in the Americas. And let every other power know that this hemisphere intends to remain the master of its own house.

To that world assembly of sovereign states, the United Nations, our last best hope in an age where the instruments of war have far outpaced the instruments of peace, we renew our pledge of support—to prevent it from becoming merely a forum for invective—to strengthen its shield of the new and the weak—and to enlarge the area in which its writ may run.

Finally, to those nations who would make themselves our adversary, we offer not a pledge but a request: that both sides begin anew the quest for peace, before the dark powers of destruction unleashed by science engulf all humanity in planned or accidental self-destruction.

We dare not tempt them with weakness. For only when our arms are sufficient beyond doubt can we be certain beyond doubt that they will never be employed.

But neither can two great and powerful groups of nations take comfort from our present course—both sides overburdened by the cost of modern weapons, both rightly alarmed by the steady spread of the deadly atom, yet both racing to alter that uncertain balance of terror that stays the hand of mankind's final war.

So let us begin anew—remembering on both sides that civility is not a sign of weakness, and sincerity is always subject to proof. Let us never negotiate out of fear. But let us never fear to negotiate.

Let both sides explore what problems unite us instead of belaboring those problems which divide us.

Let both sides, for the first time, formulate serious and precise proposals for the inspection and control of arms—and bring the absolute power to destroy other nations under the absolute control of all nations.

Let both sides seek to invoke the wonders of science instead of its terrors. Together let us explore the stars, conquer the deserts, eradicate disease, tap the ocean depths, and encourage the arts and commerce.

Let both sides unite to heed in all corners of the earth the command of Isaiah—to "undo the heavy burdens and to let the oppressed go free."

And if a beachhead of cooperation may push back the jungle

of suspicion, let both sides join in creating a new endeavor, not a new balance of power, but a new world of law, where the strong are just and the weak secure and the peace preserved.

All this will not be finished in the first 100 days. Nor will it be finished in the first 1,000 days, nor in the life of this administration, nor even perhaps in our lifetime on this planet. But let us begin.

In your hands, my fellow citizens, more than in mine, will rest the final success or failure of our course. Since this country was founded, each generation of Americans has been summoned to give testimony to its national loyalty. The graves of young Americans who answered the call to service surround the globe.

Now the trumpet summons us again—not as a call to bear arms, though arms we need; not as a call to battle, though embattled we are; but a call to bear the burden of a long twilight struggle, year in, and year out, "rejoicing in hope, patient in tribulation"—a struggle against the common enemies of man: tyranny, poverty, disease, and war itself.

Can we forge against these enemies a grand and global alliance, North and South, East and West, that can assure a more fruitful life for all mankind? Will you join in that historic effort?

In the long history of the world, only a few generations have been granted the role of defending freedom in its hour of maximum danger. I do not shrink from this responsibility—I welcome it. I do not believe that any of us would exchange places with any other people or any other generation. The energy, the faith, the devotion which we bring to this endeavor will light our country and all who serve it—and the glow from that fire can truly light the world.

30 / SENATOR FULBRIGHT COUNTERS
OLD MYTHS WITH NEW REALITIES

*The persistence of a modified Cold War psychology in the
1960's led the chairman of the Foreign Relations
Committee, Senator J. William Fulbright (1905–) of
Arkansas, to call for a sweeping reappraisal of American
policy in a Senate speech on March 25, 1964. At least
in part, this call for change was prompted by the
fact that European problems had once more faded
into the background and major challenges to American
policy were coming from the Caribbean and the Far East.*

We are confronted with a complex and fluid world situation
and we are not adapting ourselves to it. We are clinging to old
myths in the face of new realities and we are seeking to escape
the contradictions by narrowing the permissible bounds of public
discussion, by relegating an increasing number of ideas and
viewpoints to a growing category of "unthinkable thoughts." I
believe that this tendency can and should be reversed, that it is
within our ability, and unquestionably in our interests, to cut
loose from established myths and to start thinking some "unthinkable thoughts"—about the cold war and East-West relations,
about the underdeveloped countries and particularly those in
Latin America, about the changing nature of the Chinese Communist threat in Asia and about the festering war in Vietnam.

The master myth of the cold war is that the Communist bloc
is a monolith composed of governments which are not really
governments at all but organized conspiracies, divided among
themselves perhaps in certain matters of tactics, but all equally

SOURCE: *Congressional Record*, 88th Cong., 2d sess. (1964), pp. 6227–32.

resolute and implacable in their determination to destroy the free world.

I believe that the Communist world is indeed hostile to the free world in its general and long-term intentions but that the existence of this animosity in principle is far less important for our foreign policy than the great variations in its intensity and character both in time and among the individual members of the Communist bloc. Only if we recognize these variations, ranging from China, which poses immediate threats to the free world, to Poland and Yugoslavia, which pose none, can we hope to act effectively upon the bloc and to turn its internal differences to our own advantage and to the advantage of those bloc countries which wish to maximize their independence. . . .

It is not communism as a doctrine, or communism as it is practiced within the Soviet Union or within any other country, that threatens us. How the Soviet Union organizes its internal life, the gods and doctrines that it worships, are matters for the Soviet Union to determine. It is not Communist dogma as espoused within Russia but Communist imperialism that threatens us and other peoples of the non-Communist world. Insofar as a great nation mobilizes its power and resources for aggressive purposes, that nation, regardless of ideology, makes itself our enemy. Insofar as a nation is content to practice its doctrines within its own frontiers, that nation, however repugnant its ideology, is one with which we have no proper quarrel. . . .

There is little in history to justify the expectation that we can either win the cold war or end it immediately and completely. These are favored myths, respectively, of the American right and of the American left. They are, I believe, equal in their unreality and in their disregard for the feasibilities of history. We must disabuse ourselves of them and come to terms, at last, with the realities of a world in which neither good nor evil is absolute and in which those who move events and make history are those who have understood not how much but how little is within our power to change. . . .

Latin America is one of the areas of the world in which American policy is weakened by a growing divergency between old myths and new realities.

The crisis over the Panama Canal has been unnecessarily protracted for reasons of domestic politics and national pride and sensitivity on both sides—for reasons, that is, of only marginal relevance to the merits of the dispute. . . .

We Americans would do well, for a start, to divest ourselves of the silly notion that the issue with Panama is a test of our courage and resolve. I believe that the Cuban missile crisis of 1962, involving a confrontation with nuclear weapons and intercontinental missiles, was indeed a test of our courage, and we acquitted ourselves extremely well in that instance. I am unable to understand how a controversy with a small and poor country, with virtually no military capacity, can possibly be regarded as a test of our bravery and will to defend our interests. . . .

The problem of Cuba is more difficult than that of Panama, and far more heavily burdened with the deadweight of old myths and prohibitions against "unthinkable thoughts." I think the time is overdue for a candid reevaluation of our Cuban policy even though it may also lead to distasteful conclusions.

There are and have been three options open to the United States with respect to Cuba: First, the removal of the Castro regime by invading and occupying the island; second, an effort to weaken and ultimately bring down the regime by a policy of political and economic boycott; and finally, acceptance of the Communist regime as a disagreeable reality and annoyance but one which is not likely to be removed in the near future because of the unavailability of acceptable means of removing it.

The first option, invasion, has been tried in a halfhearted way and found wanting. . . .

The approach which we have adopted has been the second of those mentioned, an effort to weaken and eventually bring down the Castro regime by a policy of political and economic boycott. . . .

This policy, it now seems clear, has been a failure, and there is no reason to believe that it will succeed in the future. . . .

Having ruled out military invasion and blockade, and recognizing the failure of the boycott policy, we are compelled to consider the third of the three options open to us with respect to Cuba: the acceptance of the continued existence of the Castro regime as a distasteful nuisance but not an intolerable danger so long as the nations of the hemisphere are prepared to meet their obligation of collective defense under the Rio Treaty.

In recent years we have become transfixed with Cuba, making it far more important in both our foreign relations and in our domestic life than its size and influence warrant. We have flattered a noisy but minor demagog by treating him as if he were a Napoleonic menace. Communist Cuba has been a disruptive and subversive influence in Venezuela and other countries of the hemisphere, and there is no doubt that both we and our Latin American partners would be better off if the Castro regime did not exist. But it is important to bear in mind that, despite their best efforts, the Cuban Communists have not succeeded in subverting the hemisphere and that in Venezuela, for example, where communism has made a major effort to gain power through terrorism, it has been repudiated by a people who in a free election have committed themselves to the course of liberal democracy. It is necessary to weigh the desirability of an objective against the feasibility of its attainment, and when we do this with respect to Cuba, I think we are bound to conclude that Castro is a nuisance but not a grave threat to the United States and that he cannot be gotten rid of except by means that are wholly disproportionate to the objective. Cuban communism does pose a grave threat to other Latin American countries, but this threat can be dealt with by prompt and vigorous use of the established procedures of the inter-American system against any act of aggression. . . .

The policy of the United States with respect to Latin America as a whole is predicated on the assumption that social revolution can be accomplished without violent upheaval. This is the guiding principle of the Alliance for Progress and it may in time be vindicated. We are entitled to hope so and it is wise and necessary for us to do all that we can to advance the prospects of peaceful and orderly reform.

At the same time, we must be under no illusions as to the extreme difficulty of uprooting long-established ruling oligarchies without disruptions involving lesser or greater degrees of violence. . . .

I am not predicting violent revolutions in Latin America or elsewhere. Still less am I advocating them. I wish only to suggest that violent social revolutions are a possibility in countries where feudal oligarchies resist all meaningful change by peaceful means. We must not, in our preference for the democratic procedures envisioned by the Charter of Punta del Este, close our minds to the possibility that democratic procedures may fail in certain countries and that where democracy does fail violent social convulsions may occur. . . .

The Far East is another area of the world in which American policy is handicapped by the divergence of old myths and new realities. Particularly with respect to China, an elaborate vocabulary of make-believe has become compulsory in both official and public discussion. We are committed, with respect to China and other areas in Asia, to inflexible policies of long standing from which we hesitate to depart because of the attribution to these policies of an aura of mystical sanctity. It may be that a thorough reevaluation of our Far Eastern policies would lead us to the conclusion that they are sound and wise, or at least that they represent the best available options. It may be, on the other hand, that a reevaluation would point up the need for greater or lesser changes in our policies. The point is that, whatever the outcome of a rethinking of policy might be, we have been unwilling to undertake it because of the fear of many Government officials, undoubtedly well founded, that even the suggestion of new policies toward China or Vietnam would provoke a vehement public outcry.

I do not think the United States can, or should, recognize Communist China, or acquiesce in its admission to the United Nations under present circumstances. It would be unwise to do so, because there is nothing to be gained by it so long as the Peiping regime maintains its attitude of implacable hostility toward the United States. I do not believe, however, that this state of affairs is necessarily permanent. . . .

We would do well, as former Assistant Secretary Hilsman has recommended, to maintain an "open door" to the possibility of improved relations with Communist China in the future. For a start, we must jar open our minds to certain realities about

China, of which the foremost is that there really are not "two Chinas," but only one—mainland China; and that it is ruled by Communists and is likely to remain so for the indefinite future. Once we accept this fact, it becomes possible to reflect on the conditions under which it might be possible for us to enter into relatively normal relations with mainland China. . . .

The situation in Vietnam poses a far more pressing need for a reevaluation of American policy. . . . It seems clear that only two realistic options are open to us in Vietnam in the immediate future: the expansion of the conflict in one way or another, or a renewed effort to bolster the capacity of the South Vietnamese to prosecute the war successfully on its present scale. The matter calls for thorough examination by responsible officials in the executive branch; and until they have had an opportunity to evaluate the contingencies and feasibilities of the options open to us, it seems to me that we have no choice but to support the South Vietnamese Government and Army by the most effective means available. Whatever specific policy decisions are made, it should be clear to all concerned that the United States will continue to meet its obligations and fulfill its commitments with respect to Vietnam.

There, I believe, are some, although by no means all, of the issues of foreign policy in which it is essential to reevaluate long-standing ideas and commitments in the light of new and changing realities. In all the issues which I have discussed, American policy has to one degree or another been less effective than it might have been because of our national tendency to equate means with ends and therefore to attach a mythological sanctity to policies and practices which in themselves have no moral content or value except insofar as they contribute to the achievement of some valid national objective. I believe that we must try to overcome this excessive moralism, which binds us to old myths and blinds us to new realities and, worse still, leads us to regard new and unfamiliar ideas with fear and mistrust.

31 / PRESIDENT LYNDON B. JOHNSON
DEFINES AMERICA'S ROLE

*In a speech delivered at Johns Hopkins University on
April 7, 1965, and in a television address from
the White House on May 2, President Lyndon B.
Johnson (1908–   ) reaffirmed the American commitments
in Vietnam and in the Caribbean area. In essence, he
described America's Vietnam policy as essential to
the containment of China and United States action in the
Dominican Republic as a means for preventing further
Communist inroads in the Western Hemisphere.*

Vietnam is far from this quiet campus. We have no territory
there, nor do we seek any. The war is dirty and brutal and difficult. And some 400 young men—born into an America bursting
with opportunity and promise—have ended their lives on Vietnam's steaming soil.

Why must we take this painful road?

Why must this nation hazard its ease, its interest and its
power for the sake of a people so far away?

We fight because we must fight if we are to live in a world
where every country can shape its own destiny. And only in
such a world will our own freedom be finally secure.

This kind of a world will never be built by bombs and bullets.
Yet the infirmities of man are such that force must often precede
reason—and the waste of war, the works of peace.

We wish this were not so. But we must deal with the world
as it is, if it is ever to be as we wish.

SOURCE: *Vital Speeches of the Day*, XXXI (April 1965), 386–88, 450–52.
Reprinted with permission.

The world as it is in Asia is not a serene or peaceful place.

The first reality is that North Vietnam has attacked the independent nation of South Vietnam. Its object is total conquest. . . .

Over this war—and all Asia—is another reality: the deepening shadow of Communist China. The rulers in Hanoi are urged on by Peking. This is a regime which has destroyed freedom in Tibet, attacked India and been condemned by the United Nations for aggression in Korea. It is a nation which is helping the forces of violence in almost every continent. The contest in Vietnam is part of a wider pattern of aggressive purpose.

Why are these realities our concern? Why are we in South Vietnam?

We are there because we have a promise to keep. Since 1954 every American President has offered support to the people of South Vietnam. We have helped to build and we have helped to defend. Thus, over many years, we have made a national pledge to help South Vietnam defend its independence.

I intend to keep our promise.

To dishonor that pledge, to abandon this small and brave nation to its enemy—and to the terror that must follow—would be an unforgivable wrong.

We are also there to strengthen world order. Around the globe—from Berlin to Thailand—are people whose well-being rests, in part, on the belief they can count on us if they are attacked. To leave Vietnam to its fate would shake the confidence of all these people in the value of American commitment. The result would be increased unrest and instability, or even war.

We are also there because there are great stakes in the balance. Let no one think that retreat from Vietnam would bring an end to conflict. The battle would be renewed in one country and then another. The central lesson of our time is that the appetite of aggression is never satisfied. To withdraw from one battlefield means only to prepare for the next. We must say in Southeast Asia—as we did in Europe—in the words of the Bible: "Hitherto shalt thou come, but no further."

There are those who say that all our efforts there will be futile—that China's power is such it is bound to dominate all

Southeast Asia. But there is no end to that argument until all the nations of Asia are swallowed up.

There are those who wonder why we have a responsibility for the defense of freedom in Europe. World War II was fought in both Europe and Asia, and when it ended we found ourselves with continued responsibility for the defense of freedom.

Our objective is the independence of South Vietnam, and its freedom from attack. We want nothing for ourselves—only that the people of South Vietnam be allowed to guide their own country in their own way.

We will do everything necessary to reach that objective. And we will do only what is necessary. . . .

We hope that peace will come swiftly. But that is in the hands of others beside ourselves. And we must be prepared for a long, continued conflict. It will require patience as well as bravery—the will to endure as well as the will to resist. . . .

We will never be second in the search for such a peaceful settlement in Vietnam.

There may be many ways to this kind of peace: in discussion or negotiation with the governments concerned; in large groups or in small ones; in the reaffirmation of old agreements or their strengthening with new ones.

We have stated this position over and over again 50 times and more to friend and foe alike. And we remain ready, with this purpose, for unconditional discussions.

And until that bright and necessary day of peace we will try to keep conflict from spreading. We have no desire to see thousands die in battle—Asians or Americans. We have no desire to devastate that which the people of North Vietnam have built with toil and sacrifice. We will use our power with restraint and with all the wisdom we can command. But we will use it.

This war, like most wars, is filled with terrible irony. For what do the people of North Vietnam want? They want what their neighbors also desire: food for their hunger, health for their bodies and a chance to learn, progress for their country and an end to the bondage of material misery. And they would find all these things far more readily in peaceful association with others than in the endless course of battle. . . .

The ordinary men and women of North Vietnam and South Vietnam, of China and India, of Russia and America, are brave people. They are filled with the same proportions of hate and fear, of love and hope. Most of them want the same things for themselves and their families. Most of them do not want their sons to die in battle, or see the homes of others destroyed.

This can be their world yet. Man now has the knowledge— always before denied—to make this planet serve the real needs of the people who live on it. . . .

We often say how impressive power is. But I do not find it impressive. The guns and bombs, the rockets and warships, are all symbols of human failure. They are necessary symbols. They protect what we cherish. But they are witness to human folly.

A rich harvest in a hungry land is impressive.

The sight of healthy children in a classroom is impressive.

These—not mighty arms—are the achievements which the American nation believes to be impressive.

And—if we are steadfast—the time may come when all other nations will also find it so.

. . . . .

There are times in the affairs of nations when great principles are tested in an ordeal of conflict and danger. This is such a time for American nations. At stake are the lives of thousands, the liberty of the nation and the principles and the values of all the American republics, and that is why the hopes and the concern of this entire hemisphere are on this Sabbath Sunday focused on the Dominican Republic.

In the darkness of conflict and violence, revolution and confusion, it is not easy to find clear and uncloudy truths.

But certain things are clear. They require equally clear action. . . . The evidence that we have of the revolutionary movement indicates that it took a very tragic turn. Communist leaders, many of them trained in Cuba, seeing a chance to increase disorder, and to gain a foothold, joined the revolution.

They took increasing control. What began as a popular democratic revolution that was committed to democracy and social

justice moved into the hands of a band of Communist conspirators.

Many of the original leaders of the rebellion, the followers
of President Bosch, took refuge in foreign embassies, and they
are there tonight.

The American nations cannot, must not, and will not permit
the establishment of another Communist government in the
Western Hemisphere. This was the unanimous view of all the
American nations when in January, 1962, they declared, and I
quote, "the principles of Communism are incompatible with the
principles of the inter-American system." This is what our be-
loved President John F. Kennedy meant when less than a week
before his death he told us, we in this hemisphere must also
use every resource at our command to prevent the establishment
of another Cuba in this hemisphere.

This is and this will be the common action and the common
purpose of the democratic forces of the hemisphere. For the
danger is also a common danger and the principles are common
principles. So we have acted to summon the resources of this
entire hemisphere to this task. . . .

We know that many who are now in revolt do not seek a
Communist tyranny. We think it's tragic indeed that their high
motives have been misused by a small band of conspirators, who
receive their directions from abroad.

To those who fight only for liberty and justice and progress,
I want to join with the Organization of American States in saying, in appealing to you tonight to lay down your arms and to
assure you that there is nothing to fear.

The road is open to you to share in building a Dominican
Democracy and we in America are ready and anxious and willing
to help you.

Your courage and your dedication are top qualities which
your country and all the hemisphere need for the future.

You are needed to help shape that future, and neither we nor
any other nation in this hemisphere can or should take it upon
itself to ever interfere with the affairs of your country, or any
other country.

We believe that change comes, and we're glad that it does, and it should come through peaceful process.

But revolution in any country is a matter for that country to deal with. It becomes a matter calling for hemispheric action only, repeat only, when the object is the establishment of a communistic dictatorship.

Let me also make clear tonight that we support no single man or any single group of men in the Dominican Republic. Our goal is a simple one: We are there to save the lives of our citizens and to save the lives of all people.

Our goal in keeping the principles of the American system is to help prevent another Communist state in this hemisphere, and we would like to do this without bloodshed or without large-scale fighting. . . .

I know that no American serviceman wants to kill anyone. And I know that no American President wants to give an order which brings shooting and casualties and death.

But I want you to know, and I want the world to know, that as long as I am President of this country we are going to defend ourselves. We will defend our soldiers against attackers. We will honor our treaties. We will keep our commitments. We will defend our nation against all those who seek to destroy not only the United States but every free country of this hemisphere.

We do not want to bury anyone, as I have said so many times before. But we do not intend to be buried.